IN PRAISE OF WINE

IN PRAISE OF
WINE

An Offering of Hearty Toasts,
Quotations, Witticisms, Proverbs,
and Poetry throughout History

COMPILED AND EDITED BY
Joni G. McNutt

WITH A FOREWORD BY
Robert Mondavi

CAPRA PRESS
SANTA BARBARA

To Shannon Renee
with all my love.

LIBRARY OF CONGRESS CATALOGING-IN-PUBLICATION DATA

McNutt, Joni G.,
    In praise of wine : an offering of hearty toasts, quotations,
  witticisms, proverbs, and poetry throughout history / compiled
  and edited by Joni G. McNutt; foreword by Robert Mondavi.
        p.   cm.
    Includes bibliographical references (p221) and index.
    ISBN 0-88496-372-1 : $12.95
    1. Wine--Quotations, maxims, etc. 2. Wine--Poetry I. McNutt,
  Joni G., 1957-   .
  PN6084.W5I6 1993
  641.2'2--dc20   93-1886
                                                         CIP

CAPRA PRESS
Post Office Box 2068
Santa Barbara, CA 93120

Those who drink wine are healthy.
Those who possess wine are wealthy.
Those who praise wine are wise.
                    Joni G. McNutt

CONTENTS

FOREWORD

Wine in America has many adherents, and I am certainly pleased to welcome Joni G. McNutt and the readers of this book to the growing number. In its 7000-year history, wine has brought together many diverse interests and cultures, and increased the quality of life for many millions of people.

In the last decade we have seen this moderate beverage under attack by a number of individuals. For this reason we began a program—our Mission—to set the record straight about the many virtues of wine, as well as its detriments.

Wine is part of our culture, heritage, religion, and family, and it is certainly an essential part of the good life. When the complete record of wine is known, wine can play an integral role in most people's lives and enhance those lives.

I know the readers of *In Praise of Wine* will enjoy it as much as I have—and wine is my life. From the heart of the Napa Valley I welcome them to a life with wine.

ROBERT MONDAVI

PREFACE

Wine. The mere mention of the word evokes an array of images—romance, celebration, religious ceremony, tradition, elegance, and bon vivance. For thousands of years, wine has been an important part of civilizations throughout the world. From ancient Egypt and classic Greece to the present European societies, wine has played an integral role in shaping traditions and cultures. It has celebrated births and marriages, toasted kings and queens, honored gods and goddesses, and launched well over a thousand ships.

No other beverage has enjoyed such an illustrious and lengthy history. Throughout the ancient civilizations gods were created to honor wine; later cultures used wine to honor their gods. As one of nature's truly "natural" beverages, wine was viewed as a mystery because no one understood the process whereby the juice of ripe grapes evolved into "the nectar of the gods" without the intervention of humans. Surely, this heavenly elixir was a gift of the gods and, therefore, must be revered and given a place of prominence within society.

Wine became the sacred beverage of many cultures. Ancient Egypt worshipped the wine god, Osiris, who was also the god of life-after-death. The Egyptians so valued wine that great numbers of earthenware jars full of wine were placed in the pharaohs' tombs to accompany them on their spirit journeys to the heavens. Dionysus, the Greek god of wine, was regaled in annual spring festivals which celebrated the gift of wine. The Romans had similar fetes in honor of their wine god, Bacchus, as did the Etruscans for the god Fufluns.

The worship of the wine gods slowly vanished with the advent of Christianity, but wine had already been firmly established within the Jewish culture and, therefore, easily carried over into the religious rituals of Judeo-Christian cultures.

Until relatively recently, wine maintained its status throughout the world as a sacred beverage, albeit an alcoholic one. Here in the United States, however, even with our history of richly diverse cultures which prominently incorporated wine in their traditions and sacred rituals, wine suffered a fatal fall from grace. This is one of the few modern societies where wine is not an integral part of the culture for the majority of the populace.

Although this continent was dubbed "Vinland" upon its discovery by Leif Ericsson, the native grapevines which our forefathers found flourishing here with wild abandon were of a different species than the European varieties. Wines produced from our *vitis labrusca* grapes tasted very different from those with which they were familiar, and were not to their liking. In an attempt to produce wines in the tradition of their European heritages, cuttings of *vitis vinifera* vines were brought to the New World and transplanted. Unfortunately, the climate of the East Coast proved too rigorous for them and they perished. Wines were brought over from Europe, but did not fare well on the long journey by sailing ships. Beer and cider, which could easily be produced in the New World, soon replaced wine as the traditional beverages for the new Americans.

Wine enjoyed a resurgence in popularity across the continent on the West Coast as a result of the Spanish conquistadores. As the Franciscan missionaries expanded northward from Mexico, they extensively planted the *vitis vinifera* Mission grape in order to supply wine for their Catholic masses. Later, as the United States expanded westward in the 1800s, European immigrants brought their vines and winemaking skills with them. The *vinifera* vines flourished, and soon California produced world-class wines. This prosperity was short-lived, however, due to Prohibition, which forced most wineries out of business. After the repeal of the "great experiment", the wine industry was slow to recover. The American public had to be re-educated about wine, and it was not until the 1970s that the wine trade once again boomed on the West Coast and world-class wines were produced.

Unfortunately, over the past decade or so, our society has begun to move toward an attitude of "neoprohibitionism" which I feel is dangerous, particularly for wine. There is a current societal view which purports that all alcohol is harmful, regardless of how it is used. And, so I decided to write a wine book in hopes of combatting such a narrow-minded attitude. Thousands of books have been written about wines. Why do we need another one? Because this one is different. It doesn't tell you how to drink wine, how to choose a wine, how to make wine, or how to serve wine. It doesn't tell you how to do anything. Rather, this book is a companion to curl up with while you sip a glass of your favorite wine and travel throughout history and literature as thousands of years of wine appreciation unfold at your fingertips. It is a book that will take you back through time to share in the experience of nature's natural beverage, wine.

My first experience with wine occurred as a child of about six or seven when my brothers and I were allowed a small sample of nonvintage Manischewitz Concord Grape during a Thanksgiving dinner. Unfortunately, like the majority of American families, ours was not a wine-drinking one. Wine was not a part of our culture or tradition, and was consumed sparingly only at occasions such as Thanksgiving and Christmas dinners when our large family sat down to eat together in celebration of the holiday season. The wine lent to the festive atmosphere, and its ruby hues left an indelible impression on my young mind as my mother's best crystal goblets were raised in a toast all around the table.

Raising the glass to my lips, I must admit that I wasn't at all impressed with my initiation to this magnificent beverage, but I did manage to choke it down with a bit more decorum and dignity than my brother who, upon taking his first sip, promptly spit it into my mother's face. We were not offered wine at future family gatherings, and it wasn't until I was in high school that I once again deigned to try it.

This time the wine was a Boone's Farm Wild Mountain Grape, also nonvintage. I drank a whole bottle of it throughout the course of an evening at a Christmas party where everyone else was drinking beer. I was feeling pretty sophisticated for a seventeen-year-old until around midnight when I found myself outside on my hands and knees, turning a snowbank purple. Wine and I parted company for many years after that night.

I had brief encounters with it throughout college when visiting the homes of friends whose Italian or Jewish heritages incorporated wine as the traditional mealtime beverage.

However, it wasn't until I was in my late twenties that I had the opportunity to truly experience and learn about wine. I was hired as the manager of a college pub which served only beer and wine, and early in my employment discovered that I wasn't alone in my lack of wine knowledge. Most people I met knew very little about wine, so I decided to educate them, and myself.

I set up a series of wine tasting seminars which allowed my customers the opportunity to try several different wines at a very inexpensive price. These tastings were designed to be fun, unpretentious, and informal, but also educational. I bought wine books and did extensive research for each tasting so that I could provide my customers with a wealth of information about the wines and wineries which were represented. Quizzes held at the end of the tastings provided an opportunity to win prizes, but also offered an incentive for people to pay attention to what I was saying throughout the evening.

As the years went by, my research became more extensive and I became more interested in the history of wine and the winemaking process itself. The wine tastings became more informative and the customers were eager to learn. It was quite by chance that I became interested in wine literature. I happened to read the back label of a bottle of Robert Mondavi wine, and liked what it said:

> Wine has been with us since the beginning of civilization. It is the temperate, civilized, romantic mealtime beverage recommended in the Bible. Wine has been praised for centuries by statesmen, philosophers, poets, and scholars. Wine in moderation is an integral part of our culture, heritage and the gracious way of life.

In just a few short lines, Robert Mondavi had managed to sum up the entire essence of the history of wine. I read the quote aloud to my customers, who were most appreciative and raised their glasses in a salute to Mr. Mondavi.

I shared this passage several more times at wine tastings, usually whenever we were sampling a Mondavi wine. It received such an avid following from my customers that I eventually had to type it up and copy it off for them. I soon found myself at the library researching other passages in praise of wine that I might share at the tastings. As a graduate student in English, I found it a pleasant pastime.

However, my interest in wine literature came to a forefront the following year when I discovered that the federal government had ordered Robert Mondavi to remove his quote from his wine labels because they felt it "created a misleading impression." I was incensed that they could censor someone's freedom of speech so easily, and solely because they felt the passage was "pro-wine."

Well, what's wrong with being pro-wine? Many famous people throughout history have been pro-wine. Jesus Christ is the first example who comes to mind. And let's not forget Socrates, Aristotle, Plato, George Washington, Benjamin Franklin, Thomas Jefferson, and many others.

That's what this book is all about. It's a collection of wine literature—various types of literature which have been written in praise of wine over thousands of years.

I have tried to encompass as much wine literature as possible, but there are certain to be omissions. I have also tried to provide the author and the work cited for each piece. Unfortunately, this was not always possible to do, and some quotations were too good to pass up, so I have included them. I hope that you, dear reader, enjoy this book and learn from it. *In vino veritas.* Cheers!

Joni G. McNutt
Fairbanks, Alaska
August 1992

ACKNOWLEDGMENTS

Compiling this book was often a solitary pastime as I spent long hours in the library researching literature, and even longer hours in front of the computer typing and editing. However, this venture would never have seen fruition without the encouragement and support of many people.

I would like especially to thank Professor John Murray, my advisor, and Professor Claus Naske, who never lost faith in me and helped me jump through several "hoops"; the staff of the Elmer E. Rasmuson Library at the University of Alaska Fairbanks for doing such a great job of procuring interlibrary loan books for me; the staff of Wood Center at UAF for offering support, understanding, friendship, and the use of their computers; Kate Wattum for her printing expertise and advice; Marian Taylor for accompanying me to Napa and Sonoma; Professor Joe Dupras for his advice; Jeri and Howard Maxwell for their support; Gail Adams for her computer expertise; Arna Dan Isacsson and Ami Gjestson for Alaska Highway wine and campfires; Becki Darling for her support and her couch; my alma mater, Westbrook College, for its kind assistance; and my mother for allowing me that first taste of wine.

I am also immensely indebted to the many authors throughout history who have written so eloquently on the topic of wine—this book could not exist without their contributions. Lastly, and most importantly, I would like to thank the many friends who have enhanced my life by sharing their love and appreciation of wine with me—to each of you I raise my glass. Thank you.

INTRODUCTION

From earliest times, wine has been an integral component of humanity's artistic, cultural, and religious activities. Although the Egyptian was not the first civilization to make wine, it was the first to record and celebrate the details of its winemaking skills. The Hearst, Ebers, and London Papyruses, circa 1550 B.C., all refer to wine used for medicinal purposes, while the Harris Papyrus, the longest papyrus roll which survives from ancient Egypt, indicates that Ramses III offered vast quantities of wine to the gods and their temples.

> I made vineyards without limit for you in the southern oasis and the northern oasis as well, and others in great numbers in the southern region.

His benediction to the god Amon not only recounts the hundreds of thousands of vineyards which were dedicated to the deity, but establishes wine as one of the oldest of literary topics. Wine has occupied a prominent place in the literature of every age since.

The Christian Bible contains numerous references to wine. In fact, in the Old Testament, only the Book of Jonah makes no mention of it. During Biblical times, one of wine's predominant uses was as a medicine, as prescribed by St. Paul when he suggested "use a little wine for thy stomach's sake and thine often infirmities." However, wine was regarded primarily as a benevolent gift to humankind from God. Genesis, the first book of the Bible, states, "Therefore God gave thee of the dew of heaven, and the fatness of the earth, and plenty of corn and wine." A similar sentiment is expressed in the Book of Isaiah:

> And in this mountain shall the Lord of hosts make unto all people a feast of fat things, a feast of wines on the lees, of fat things full of marrow, of wines on the lees well refined.

The Books of Proverbs, Psalms, and, most especially, Ecclesiastes, all contain passages referring to wine as a gift

19

from God. In addition, wine during Biblical times was regarded as a tonic to soothe humankind's troubled souls and weary minds, as evidenced in the following passage from the Book of Proverbs:

> Give strong drink unto him that is ready to perish, and wine unto those that be of heavy hearts. Let him drink, and forget his poverty, and remember his misery no more.

As with most ancient and modern religions, wine was also used as a sacred beverage to be consumed in tribute to God. The Book of Numbers illustrates this practice with the passage: "In the holy place shalt thou cause the strong wine to be poured unto the Lord for a drink offering"

The Bible also reinforced an important literary contribution regarding both wine and the grapevine as allegorical symbols. This symbolism was carried over from the Greek and Roman civilizations, which had used the allegories extensively. The Books of Nehemiah, Jeremiah, Ezekial, Joel, Amos, and Zechariah all contain passages which depict the vine in symbolic terms, but the most famous quote is from the Gospel of John, where Jesus says:

> I am the true vine, and my Father is the husbandman. Every branch in me that beareth not fruit he taketh away. . . . As the branch cannot bear fruit of itself, except it abide in the vine; no more can ye abide in me. I am the vine, ye are the branches.

Additional passages in the New Testament, which describes the life and teachings of Jesus Christ, pay homage to wine. Jesus performed his first miracle at the wedding feast of Cana with the "water that was made wine." Later, at the Last Supper, Christ instructed his disciples to drink of his cup of wine, "or this is my blood of the new testament, which is shed for many for the remission of sins." Throughout history Christians have consumed communion wine as an atonement in remembrance of him.

Many other religious writings contain references to wine

and sing its praises as a medicine, a sacred beverage, and a gift to benefit humankind. The Babylonian Talmud says that "where wine is lacking, drugs are necessary" and that "wine will make a man intelligent." Wine is a vital part of Jewish culture and tradition. Jewish religious laws and literature detail the joy of wine and the integral role it plays in communal and family life, as well as in worship.

Ancient writings from India, circa 2000 B.C. - 1000 A.D., mention that wine was worshipped as both a god and a powerful medicine; and ancient Chinese writings describe wine being used medicinally, as well as in sacrificial rituals during the Chang and Chou Dynasties, circa 1100 - 250 B.C.

However, ancient Greek civilization did the most to enhance wine's prominence in literature. Greek literature placed wine upon a literary pedestal and devoted odes, poems, plays, and entire philosophies to this nectar of the gods. Although the Greeks did use wine as a functional beverage in the areas of medicine and religion, within their culture wine became more of an aesthetic beverage and was romanticized for its mysterious powers and benefits.

Both *The Iliad* and *The Odyssey* are full of references about wine, describing it as "rich," "divine," "a rare nectar," and "worthy of the gods." These epic poems also contain lengthy passages about wine's use as a medicine, both internally and externally, which has caused some historians to suggest that Homer was a learned physician, as well as a lyric poet. He describes wine as an antiseptic, a sedative, and a staple food.

The Greek philosopher Socrates also recognized the benefits of wine, but described them more ethereally:

> Wine moistens and tempers the spirits, and lulls the cares of the mind to rest. . . . It revives our joys, and is oil to the dying flame of life. If we drink temperately, and small draughts at a time, the wine distills into our lungs like sweetest morning dew. . . . It is then the wine commits no rape upon our reason, but pleasantly invites us to agreeable mirth.

Plato reflects a similar attitude in declaring that "wine is a remedy for the moroseness of old age." Euripides devoted an entire play, appropriately entitled *The Bacchae*, to wine and to Bacchus, the god of wine. In fact, the annual springtime festivals which celebrated the cult of Dionysus, as Bacchus was also known, resulted in the construction of the very first theatre as early as the sixth century B.C.

Homer, Theognis, Alcaeus, Aeschylus, Simonides, Pindar, Bacchylides, Socrates, Plato, Antiphanes, and Euripides all sang the praises of wine, but the most dedicated and prolific oenophile of that era was Anacreon. A lyric poet, he wrote numerous odes which celebrated wine and love in simple verse.

> Wine gives a kind release from care,
> And courage to subdue the fair;
> Instructs the cheerful to advance
> Harmonious in the sprightly dance,
> Hail! goblet rich with generous wines!

Anacreon saw wine as an enhancement to life, a means to an end. It released him from care and woe, invoked the heavenly muse, gave courage and strength, and, most particularly, inspired love.

Wine's use as a medicinal agent flourished during this period. Hesiod wrote of wine as a nutrient and tonic, and Alcaeus described wine as the best remedy for fatigue, distress, and pain. However, the greatest advancement of wine as a medicine was due to Hippocrates, who gave the field of medicine its code of ethics. He used wine as a therapeutic treatment for practically everything.

The literature of ancient Rome followed the Greek example, devoting much writing to the topic of wine. Wine continued to be used medicinally, and, again, poets, playwrights, and philosophers immortalized the beverage, extolling its many virtues through innumerable odes. Virgil, Horace, and Ovid…the greatest poets of their time…all wrote extensively on the topic. Virgil and Horace, apparently both zealous oenophiles, not only sang the praises of wine in general, but of specific wines and varietals which were common to that region and day. Falernian wine in particular received a great deal of commendations and was a favorite of

Horace, as evidenced in the following passage:

> Why not at ease beneath this pine
> Our whitening hair with roses twine,
> And quaff the rich Falernian wine?

Wine was not only becoming more specific as a literary topic, it was becoming more specialized overall. It was during the Roman period that winemaking and viticulture began to be studied and written about. Although there are Biblical references offering advice on planting vines and cultivating the vine in Palestine, Cato the Elder wrote the first detailed book about viticulture during the second century B.C.

This opened a new realm of wine literature. Now wine was a primary topic of agricultural literature, as well as medical, religious, and poetical. Cato could be considered the author of the first "how-to" book about wine. Little did he know of the precedent he set. His work is of tremendous significance to the field of winemaking, and of considerable interest to the field of literature as it is the oldest prose work in the Latin language.

Columella and Pliny the Elder, contemporaries during the first century A.D., both wrote extensive treatises on farming which systematically detailed the various techniques of cultivating grapevines. Columella's work consisted of twelve volumes known as *De Re Rustica*, and is considered the most comprehensive of all the Roman works regarding agriculture. The third, fourth, and fifth volumes are specifically devoted to the cultivation of the vine, as well as other fruit trees, while the twelfth volume addresses winemaking. *De Re Rustica* also outlines the different medical effects of specific grape varieties, and examines the economics of wine production.

Pliny's work, *Naturalis Historia*, devotes twelve volumes exclusively to medicine, specifically outlining the therapeutic benefits of wine. In addition, Pliny details Roman viticultural techniques, mentioning close to two hundred different grape varieties and critiquing approximately one hundred different types of wines, thereby setting yet another precedent for future wine writers.

The works of Cato, Columella, and Pliny were important to wine literature as they were the first encyclopedic books written on the various aspects of wine. In addition, they set the stage for the advancement of viticulture and winemaking by providing detailed, systematic processes for both. Pliny even set a precedent by denouncing wine snobbery when he said, "The best kind of wine is that which is most pleasant to him who drinks it." But perhaps he is most famous for his phrase, "In vino veritas", which has lived on through the millennia as the philosophical creed of wine lovers around the world, and given Roman wine culture a lasting place in literary history.

Throughout the second and third centuries, wine continued to be used extensively as a medicine. Both Galen and Athenaeus wrote about wine's numerous functions as a therapeutic agent. Galen's work, entitled *De Antidotis*, was especially important to the literature of wine because it was the first to classify wine by various types and regions. It also delineated the chemical characteristics and physiological effects of various wines, thereby essentially turning the art of healing into a science.

During the fourth century, when the Roman capital transferred to Byzantium (present-day Turkey), the center of world culture and learning was displaced. As a result, wine literature from the period of the Middle Ages, circa 475 - 1450, is somewhat scarce. The only major work of significance made by Roman civilization during this time was *Liber de Vinis*. Written by Arnaldus de Villanova toward the end of the thirteenth century, it listed forty-nine different medicinal wines and their benefits.

The majority of literature written in praise of wine during the Middle Ages appeared in the Chinese, Persian, and Japanese cultures. There were many Chinese poets who wrote about wine, but the most renowned is Li Po, who composed simple philosophical poems dealing with wine, love, and nature.

> Riches and poverty, long or short life,
> By the maker of things are proportioned and disposed;
> But a cup of wine levels life and death
> And a thousand things obstinately hard to prove.

The most noted Persian poet singing the praises of wine was, of course, Omar Khayyam, whose work, "The Rubaiyat", has delighted wine lovers and scholars since the eleventh century. Composed in quatrains, the long poem speaks of love, and wine, and life. Its most famous passage is:

> A Book of Verses underneath the Bough,
> A Jug of Wine, a Loaf of Bread…and Thou
> Beside me singing in the Wilderness…
> Oh, Wilderness were Paradise enow.

A later Persian poet, by about three hundred years, named Hafiz, also wrote in praise of wine and espoused a similar, although more solitary, sentiment when he wrote:

> A book of verses and a cup of pure wine,
> Are truly your most intimate friends.
> Watch your road for it has curves and bends;
> Enjoy wine for only once is life thine.

The early Japanese culture's most renowned poet of wine during this era was Yoshida Kenko. He extolled the virtues of this magnificent beverage in his *Essays in Idleness*, claiming that "on a moonlit night, a morning after a snowfall, or under the cherry blossoms, it adds to our pleasure if, while chatting at our ease, we bring forth the wine cups." Kenko's poetry illustrates his appreciation of the enhancement wine can add to one's life.

A few decades later, Chaucer, writing in England, did not disagree in the least. The son of a vintner, he was no stranger to wine, and also appreciated the benefits wine had to offer humankind.

> He seyde:
> I see well it is necessarie,
> Where that we goon, good wyn with us carie
> For that wol turne rancour and disese
> T'accord and love, and many a wrong apese.

As civilization climbed out of the Dark Ages and into the Renaissance, so, too, did wine literature. The spread of Christianity and the monasteries during the Middle Ages had encouraged the spread of winemaking as well. Wine was more readily available to more people, and, with the advent of Gutenberg's first printing press in 1453, wine literature was well on its way to becoming an established realm. In fact, Arnaldus' *Liber de Vinis* was the first wine book to be published, and became an instant best-seller, appearing in at least twenty-one editions.

The Renaissance brought a revival of art, literature, and learning based upon the classical sources of Greece and Rome. During this time, many of the writings of the ancient poets and philosophers were unearthed, translated, and published for the first time. The wine literature of the ancient civilizations enjoyed a resurgence of popularity not known even during its own epoch.

Because of this newfound interest in the classical literature, European wine literature of the Renaissance consisted mostly of translations of the Greek and Roman works which had been written centuries before. A few authors ventured forth with new praise of wine, but none compared with England's most illustrious and prolific playwright and poet, William Shakespeare. His comedies, tragedies, and poems dominated the wine literature of this period.

An avid oenophile himself, Shakespeare incorporated some mention of some type of wine into virtually each of the thirty-seven plays he wrote. His most famous tribute is to sack, the Elizabethan term for sherry, which Falstaff delivers in *Henry IV*. As with many of Shakespeare's writings, certain passages about wine have become renowned almost to the point of being cliches. Examples of such quotes include: "Good wine is a good familiar creature, if it be well us'd; exclaim no more against it," from *Othello*, and "Good wine needs no bush," from *As You Like It*. This element of cliche reinforces the impact which Shakespeare's work had as an element of wine literature. Perhaps no other single author ever did more to advance the praise of wine to the general populace throughout history.

The Neoclassical Period, which followed, also benefited the literature of wine. The very first mention of champagne in English literature was made in 1663 in Samuel Butler's "Hudibras":

> I'll carve your name on barks of trees
> With True-Love-Knots, and flourishes,
> That shall infuse eternal spring
> And everlasting flourishing
> Drink every letter o' it in stum,
> And make it brisk Champaign become.

Having recently been discovered, champagne was a popular topic, and authors such as George Etherege, George Farquhar, and Francois Voltaire mentioned it, as did the emperor, Napoleon I. Many of the Neoclassical poets devoted their verses to wine, as well as Bacchus, the god of wine. Alexander Brome praised the particular virtues of claret and canary, and Henry Carey immortalized port, but the greatest tribute during this period was John Gay's long poem entitled simply, "Wine, A Poem." The poem, a parody of Milton's *Paradise Lost*, is essentially an argument which supports wine in regard to literature. Gay's primary contention is that wine, being a gift of God, has divine powers which invoke the heavenly muses, thereby inspiring the poet to greater heights of insight and achievement which he would not otherwise attain. He expressed it, thusly:

> BACCHUS Divine, aid my adventurous Song,
> That with no middle flight intends to soar
> Inspir'd, Sublime on Pegasean Wing
> By thee upborn, I draw Miltonic Air.

Other important contributions during the Neoclassical Period came from some of our American forefathers, who advocated the use of wine, recognized its benefits to human-kind, and encouraged its cultivation. Benjamin Franklin, George Washington, and Thomas Jefferson were all ardent oenophiles, and both Washington and Jefferson grew grape-vines on their plantations. In fact, Jefferson was an avid student of oenology and devoted much time to traveling throughout Europe and learning more about the winemak-ing processes. He kept detailed notebooks about his purchases of wines and vines from abroad, as well as meticulous notes on his own trials with making wine in the eastern United States.

An early supporter of the potential American wine industry, Jefferson felt that the United States could "make as great a variety of wines as are made in Europe, not exactly the same kinds, but doubtless as good." Little did he know how prophetic his statement was.

While the American wine industry flourished in the nineteenth century, American wine literature did not fare as well during that same time frame, known as the Romantic Era. England dominated literature with such illustrious literary names as Byron, Keats, and Shelley--all of whom also happened to write about wine, and were rather prolific on the subject. Byron's *Don Juan* praised the "immortal rain" of champagne, Keats devoted his "Lines on the Mermaid Tavern" to the virtues of fine canary, and Shelley romanticized "the exultation and the joy of Bacchus."

Although not as widely represented, the American poets made a strong showing through the works of Emerson, Longfellow, and Poe. Emerson expressed his feelings about the divine, restorative powers of wine in his poem dedicated to Bacchus:

> Pour, Bacchus! the remembering wine;
> Retrieve the loss of me and mine!
> Vine for vine be antidote,
> And the grape requite the lote!
> Haste to cure the old despair,...
> Reason in Nature's lotus drenched,
> The memory of ages quenched;
> Give them again to shine;
> Let wine repair what this undid;
> And where the infection slid,
> A dazzling memory revive;
> Refresh the faded tints,
> Recut the aged prints,
> And write my old adventures with the pen
> Which on the first day drew,
> Upon the tablets blue,
> The dancing Pleiads and eternal men.

Longfellow was more specific and chose the American

wine, catawba, as his poetic inspiration. This was an important milestone in American wine literature because it was the first major literary work to honor a grape variety of the *vitis labrusca* species, which grew wild in the eastern United States, but was not known for producing wines of any outstanding character. Perhaps Longfellow was a better poet than wine connoisseur.

Poe certainly was. Most wine lovers, upon reading Poe's famous short story, "The Cask of Amontillado", immediately recognize that he was not very well-versed in the world of wine. When he states that one of the characters of the story would not know the difference between amontillado and sherry, Poe makes a major faux-pas; amontillado is a type of sherry. In spite of the misinformation, "The Cask of Amontillado" is still popular, and in that respect it has benefited wine by exposing a wider populace to the subject.

American wine literature came into prominence in the early twentieth century, which is unusual in light of the "great experiment" of Prohibition. Perhaps that was the inspiration of many of the lesser-known poets and writers whose sole literary achievements came as devotees of Bacchus. They were numerous during that time, but their numbers paled greatly in comparison to the literary giants of the period who also happened to be great oenophiles, writers such as Ernest Hemingway.

Hemingway's novels are replete with wine references, paying the beverage an homage as only he could. The following passage from *Death in the Afternoon* best illustrates his passionate love of wine:

> Wine is one of the most civilized things in the world and one of the natural things of the world that has been brought to the greatest perfection, and it offers a greater range of enjoyment and appreciation than, possibly, any other purely sensory thing which may be purchased.

Authors from other countries were equally eloquent in their praise of wine, and wine literature flourished during the twentieth century. Saintsbury, Henley, Belloc, and Armstrong all devoted works of literature to the topic. George Saintsbury's famous *Notes on a Cellar-Book* became a classic handbook for modern oenophiles, extolling the many virtues of wine and arguing against the irrational sentiments of the prohibitionists. He recognized the benefits of wine and claimed that "when [the wines] were good they pleased my senses, cheered my spirits, improved my moral and intellectual powers, besides enabling me to confer the same benefits on other people."

Ernest Henley's poem, "The Spirit of Wine", also lauds the aesthetic values of the divine beverage. In it, wine sings its own praises:

> Inspiration in essence,
> I am wisdom and wit to the wise,
> His visible muse to the poet,
> The soul of desire to the lover,
> The genius of laughter to all.

The greatest compliment paid to wine during the twentieth century, however, was by the Anglo-French poet, Hilaire Belloc, who composed a heroic poem in its honor. The opening stanza outlines the poem's intent while invoking the heavenly muse to assist in the celebration of wine:

> To exalt, enthrone, establish and defend,
> To welcome home mankind's mysterious friend:
> Wine, true begetter of all arts that be;
> Wine, privilege of the completely free;
> Wine the recorder; wine the sagely strong;
> Wine, bright avenger of sly-dealing wrong,
> Awake Ausonian Muse, and sing the vineyard song!

Other works of literature during this time glorified wine less poetically, but just as eloquently. It was during the modern age that wine writing developed into a literary field of its own. Suddenly there was an influx of wine books. These books not only instructed the public in the fine arts of growing vines and making wines, as had the ancient books of Cato, Columella, and Pliny, but told them how to choose the right wines for dinner, how to read a wine label, how to buy wine, how to store wine, how to open wine, how to serve wine, how to taste wine, and even how to appreciate wine.

The twentieth century has witnessed the proliferation of the "wine writer", that peculiar breed of author whose primary occupation is to write about wine. It's a tough job, but someone has to do it. These writers are not poets, playwrights, novelists, or essayists who happen to occasionally use wine as a literary subject during their careers, nor are they philosophers, doctors, or statesmen praising the favorable aspects of wine. Rather, they are authors who, through their in-depth research of the subject and their undying passion for the beverage, enhance the public's awareness and appreciation of wine. Andre L. Simon, H. Warner Allen, Clifton Fadiman, and Hugh Johnson are some of the foremost wine writers, critics, and authorities of the modern era.

Their individual areas of oeneological expertise and passion encompass a wide spectrum and include: the history of wine, specific varietals of wine, particular wine-producing regions or countries, viticulture, the wine-making process and its technology, the critiquing and rating of wines, the aesthetics of wine, and the literature of wine. While wine books are primarily designed to be informative and educational, most are also extremely pleasurable to read.

In his book entitled *Drink*, Andre L. Simon says that wine "releases the brakes of [a person's] self-consciousness and softens the hard-baked crust of dust so that the seeds below may send forth sweet flowers." H. Warner Allen offers a similar viewpoint in *The Wines of France*:

> Great wine is a work of art. It produces a harmony of pleasing sensations, which appeal directly to the aesthetic sense, and at the same time sharpens the wit, gladdens the heart, and stimulates all that is most generous in human nature.

Clifton Fadiman is just as poetically passionate in *The Joys of Wine*:

> Wine is alive, and when you offer it to your fellow man you are offering him life. More than that you are

calling out more life in him, you are engaging in what might be called a creative flattery, for you are asking him to summon up his powers of discrimination, to exercise his taste, or perhaps merely to evince curiosity or a desire to learn. I know of no other liquid that, placed in the mouth, forces one to think.

And, in his book, *Wine*, Hugh Johnson embraces the philosophy that "wine has the most precious quality that art has: it makes ideas, people, incidents, places, sensations seem larger than life."

Each of these wine writers possesses a love of wine that is evident in their literature. They not only appreciate the aesthetic qualities which wine has to offer, but realize its immense historical and cultural significance, as well.

From the ancient Egyptian hieroglyphics to the most recently-released wine book, literature has expressed our cultures' sentiments about wine and its mystical powers. Poets, philosophers, and kings have all sung its praises, and in doing so have not only ensured wine a prominent place in history and literature, but in our hearts and souls, as well.

From Homer to Hemingway, Sophocles to Shakespeare, and Anacreon to Armstrong, we raise our glasses in a toast to each of those who has ever found pleasure over a bottle of wine, and felt the incessant need to share that joy with the rest of the world by invoking the heavenly muses. Salut!

WINE

IN

ANCIENT

CIVILIZATIONS

(c. 3000 B.C. - c. 475 A.D.)

WINE IS AS OLD AS HISTORY. It has been an important part of cultures and civilizations for thousands of years, the earliest evidence of winemaking dating back 8000 years to the Stone Age known as Neolithic B. The oldest existing evidence of grapevine cultivation dates from 700-5000 B.C. from the area recently known as Soviet Georgia.

No one knows exactly how the discovery of wine came about, but popular theories hold that it was an accident. One of our ancient ancestors gathered some grapes, stored them in an earthenware container of some sort, and after a short period of time discovered that the weight of the fruit had crushed some of the grapes. Fermentation was induced naturally when the yeast on the outside of the skins came into contact with the sugar of the juice inside.

The people liked what they tasted, and soon began crushing the grapes to enhance the fermentation process. As experimentation continued, the art of winemaking was born, and wine was well on its way to becoming an integral part of human culture.

Evidence of wine exists in virtually every ancient civilization throughout the world. The technology of winemaking was mastered 3000-5000 years ago. Egyptian hieroglyphics vividly depict scenes of grape harvests and other viticultural tasks. In fact, every aspect of winemaking, from harvest to fermentation, is recorded in the paintings of the royal tombs. Similar information is contained in the writing tablets uncovered in Assyria, Carthage, Tunis, and Morocco. Mesopotamian, Babylonian, and ancient Chinese civilizations all knew the art of making wine.

Recently, archaeologists uncovered the ruins of a 2600-year-old winery near Palestine, and additional findings at the Godin Tepe site in Iran offer evidence that the ancient civilizations of the Near East were making wine as far back as 3500 B.C. The oldest physical evidence of wine used as a medicine is a prescription on a clay tablet unearthed from the ruins of Nippur, an ancient Sumerian city which existed around 2500 B.C. Wine was also used extensively in religious services as an offering to the gods.

The process of making wine has changed very little since the days of these ancient civilizations. Pictographs and hieroglyphics show that vines were grown on trellises, and the individual plants were watered by hand. During harvest, the grapes were picked into baskets, placed in shallow troughs, and treaded to crush them. The wine was then poured into open earthenware jars to ferment. Earthenware jars, called amphorae, were also used for storage, but were sealed with rushes and mud to allow the wine to age.

The Egyptians recognized that wine did improve with age, and often labeled the jars in detail, listing the vintage, the vineyard, and winemaker. Many of these jars have been found in the royal tombs of the pharaohs. King Tut's tomb contained approximately three dozen amphorae; unfortunately, the wine had long since evaporated.

With the westward march of civilization, wine was transplanted from the Near East into Europe. The first Europeans to grow grapes were the Greeks, who then extended the cultivation of the grapevine throughout the Mediterranean to places such as Rome.

Wine was revered in both civilizations. The Greeks worshipped the wine god, Dionysus, and the Romans, Bacchus. Vineyards were dedicated to deities, and special celebrations were held in honor of wine. In Rome, wine was considered of such great value that it was used as a currency for barter and trade.

Both the Greeks and the Romans used wine medicinally and in religious ceremonies, as well as in everyday life. It was an integral part of their cultures. However, wine was rarely consumed straight. It was mixed with water in order to extend the supply and to enable people to drink for longer periods of time without ill effects. Other things were added to wine besides water...spices, aromatics, honey, raisins, saffron, mint, sea water, rose petals, pepper, violets, and resin were all common ingredients. The Romans even made a smoked wine.

The technology during this time changed little from the earlier Eastern winemaking practices. Wine was primarily still stored in earthenware containers, but barrels began to be used around the first century B.C. The earliest pictorial representation of a barrel is on Trajan's Column (c. 113 A.D.), which shows Roman soldiers loading barrels of wine onto a boat.

In fact, Rome's soldiers significantly promoted the propagation of the grapevine. They carried vines with them on their journeys, planting them in their newly-conquered lands. Rome is thus responsible for spreading viticulture throughout most of Europe, which has become the greatest wine-producing region of the world.

This is the wine-cellar,
the place for the produce of the vine is in it.
One is merry in it.
And the heart of him who goes forth from it rejoices.

INSCRIPTION IN AN EGYPTIAN WINE CELLAR IN ESNA
(c. 2500 B.C.)

I made vineyards without limit for you in the southern oasis and the northern oasis as well, and others in great numbers in the southern region. I multiplied them in the north in the hundreds of thousands. I equipped them with vintners, with captives of foreign lands and with canals from my digging, that were supplied with lotuses and with sdh-wine and wine like water for presentation before you in victorious Thebes.

RAMSES III: *address to the god Amon in the Harris Papyrus*
(c. 1198-1167 B.C.)

Therefore God gave thee of the dew of heaven, and the fatness of the earth, and plenty of corn and wine.

GENESIS 27:28, *Old Testament*
(c. 8th century B.C.)

In the holy place shalt thou cause the strong wine to be poured unto the Lord for a drink offering.

NUMBERS 28:7, *Old Testament*
(c. 8th century B.C.)

And the vine said unto them, should I leave my wine, which cheereth God and man, and go to be promoted over the trees?

JUDGES 9:13, *Old Testament*

Give strong drink unto him that is ready to perish, and wine unto those that be of heavy hearts. Let him drink, and forget his poverty, and remember his misery no more.

PROVERBS 31:6-7

And behold joy and gladness, slaying oxen, and killing sheep, eating flesh, and drinking wine: let us eat and drink; for tomorrow we shall die.

> ISAIAH 22:13, *Old Testament*
> (c. 8th century)

There is a crying for wine in the streets; all joy is darkened, the mirth of the land is gone.

> ISAIAH 24:11

And in this mountain shall the Lord of hosts make unto all people a feast of fat things, a feast of wines on the lees, of fat things full of marrow, of wines on the lees well refined.

> ISAIAH 25:6

Wine gives strength to weary men.

> HOMER: *The Iliad*
> Greek epic poet (8th century B.C.)

Satisfy your hearts with food and wine, for therein is courage and strength.

> HOMER: *The Iliad*

He fetched me gifts of varied excellence;
. . . but his gift most famed
Was twelve great vessels, filled with such rich wine
As was incorruptible and divine.
He kept it as his jewel, of which none knew
But he himself, his wife and him that drew. . .
A sacred odour berthed about the bowl.
Had you the odour smelt and sent it cast,
It would have vexed you to forbear the taste.
But then the taste gain'd too, the spirit it brought
To dare things high set up on end my thought.

> HOMER: *The Odyssey*

. . . lined along the wall, the great jars standing up, full of a rare nectar, a wine worthy of the gods, mellowed by age and as sweet as honey.

> HOMER: *The Odyssey*

And wine can of the wise their wits beguile,
Make the sage frolic, and the serious smile.

> HOMER

Wine is a magician, for it loosens the tongue and liberates good stories.

> HOMER

The gods made wine the best thing for mortal man to scatter cares.

> STASINUS OF CYPRUS: *The Cypria*
> Greek epic poet (7th century B.C.)

The firstfruit also of thy corn, of thy wine, and of thine oil, and the first of the fleece of thy sheep, shalt thou give him.

> DEUTERONOMY 18:4, *Old Testament*
> (c. 721-late 5th century B.C.)

The wine urges me on, bewitching wine, which sets even a wise man singing and laughing.
Fire proves the treasures of the mine,
The soul of man is proved by wine.

> THEOGNIS
> Greek poet (6th century B.C.)

Thou hast made us to drink the wine of astonishment.

> PSALMS 60:3, *Old Testament*
> (c. 5th-6th century B.C.)

40

For in the hand of the Lord there is a cup, and the wine is red.

PSALMS 75:8

He causeth the grass to grow for the cattle, and herb for the service of man: that he may bring forth food out of the earth; and wine that maketh glad the heart of man, and oil to make his face to shine, and bread which strengtheneth man's heart.

PSALMS 104:14-15

Let us drink the juice divine,
The gift of Bacchus, god of wine.

ANACREON: *Fragments*
Greek lyric poet and oenophile (c. 582-485 B.C.)

When I drink wine
My pain is driven away
And my dark thoughts
Fly to the ocean winds.

ANACREON: *Fragments*

Today I'll haste to quaff my wine
As if tomorrow ne'er should shine;
And if tomorrow comes, why then—
I'll haste to quaff my wine again.
And thus while all our days are bright,
Nor time has dimmed their bloomy light,
Let us the festal hours beguile
With mantling cup and cordial smile;
And shed from every bowl of wine
The richest drop on Bacchus' shrine.
For Death may come with brow unpleasant,
May come when least we wish him present,
And beckon to the sable shore
And grimly bid us—drink no more.

ANACREON: *Ode VIII*

Observe when Mother Earth is dry
She drinks the drippings of the sky;
And then the dewy cordial gives
To every thirsty plant that lives.
The vapors, which at evening weep
Are beverage to the swelling deep,
And when the rosy sun appears,
He drinks the ocean's misty tears.
The moon, too, quaffs her paly stream
Of lustre from the solar beam;
Then hence with all your sober thinking!
Since Nature's holy law is drinking;
I'll make the law of Nature mine,
And pledge the Universe in wine.

ANACREON: *Ode XXI*

When wine I quaff, before my eyes
Dreams of poetic glory rise;
And, freshen'd by the goblet's dews,
My soul invokes the heavenly Muse.
When wine I drink, all sorrow's o'er;
I think of doubts and fears no more;
But scatter to the railing wind
Each gloomy phantom of the mind.
When I drink wine, th' ethereal boy,
Bacchus himself, partakes my joy;
And while we dance through vernal bowers,
Whose ev'ry breath comes fresh from flowers,
In wine he makes my senses swim,
Till the gale breathes nought but him!

ANACREON: *Ode L*

Then, when the ripe and vermil wine,—
Blest infant of the pregnant vine,
Which now in mellow clusters swells,—
Oh! when it bursts its roseate cells,

Brightly the joyous stream shall flow,
To balsam every mortal woe!
None shall be then cast down or weak,
For health and joy shall light each cheek;
No heart will then desponding sigh,
For wine shall bid despondence fly.
Thus—till another autumn's glow
Shall bid another vintage flow.

ANACREON: *Ode LVI*

The Happy Effects of Wine

See! see! the jolly god appears,
His hand a mighty goblet bears;
With sparkling wine full charg'd it flows,
The sovereign cure of human woes.

Wine gives a kind release from care,
And courage to subdue the fair;
Instructs the cheerful to advance
Harmonious in the sprightly dance,
Hail! goblet, rich with generous wines!
See! round the verge a vine-branch twines.
See! how the mimic clusters roll,
As ready to refill the bowl.

Wine keeps its happy patients free
From every painful malady;
Our best physician all the year;
Thus guarded, no disease we fear,
No troublesome disease of mind,
Until another year grows kind,
And loads again the fruitful vine,
And brings again our health—new wine.

ANACREON

Alas, alas, in ways so dark,
'Tis only wine can strike a spark.

ANACREON: *Fragments*

Lᴇᴛ ᴜs Dʀɪɴᴋ

Why wait we for the torches' lights?
Now let us drink, while day invites,
    In mighty flagons hither bring
The deep-red blood of many a vine,
    That we may largely quaff, and sing
The praises of the god of wine,
The son of Jove and Semele,
Who gave the jocund wine to be
    A sweet oblivion to our woes.
Fill, fill the goblet, one and two;
Let every brimmer, as it flows,
    In sportive chase the last pursue.

        Aʟᴄᴀᴇᴜs
        Greek lyric poet (6th century B.C.)

The best medicine is wine.
        Aʟᴄᴀᴇᴜs: *Fragments*

Polished brass is the mirror of the body and wine of the mind.
        Aᴇsᴄʜʏʟᴜs: *Fragments*
        Greek tragicist (525-456 B.C.)

Wine the defender against care.
        Sɪᴍᴏɴɪᴅᴇs: *Fragments*
        Greek lyric poet (556-468 B.C.)

Praise the wine that is old.
        Pɪɴᴅᴀʀ: *Olympian Odes*
        Greek lyric poet (c. 522-c. 440 B.C.)

My land produces the life-giving medicine of Dionysus for
all trouble.
        Pɪɴᴅᴀʀ: *Paens*

He that is penniless is rich, and even the wealthy find their hearts expanding when they are smitten by the arrows of the vine.

PINDAR: *Eulogies*

Wine, to a gifted bard,
Is a mount that merrily races;
From watered wits
No good has ever grown.

CRATINUS
Greek comic poet (c. 519-423 B.C.)

Wine that cheers the heart and rules the world.

ION OF CHIOS: *Dithyrambs*
Greek poet (5th century B.C.)

Wine, though bitter, sweetens all bitterness.

MOSES IBN EZRA: *Selected Poems*
Hebrew scribe and priest (5th century B.C.)

Sweet compulsion flowing from the wine. . . warms the heart, and hope of Love returned, all mingled with the gifts of Dionysus darts through the brain, sending the thoughts of men to heights supreme. Straightway it overthrows the battlements of cities, and every man dreams that he is heir to a throne. With gold, yea, and ivory, his house is gleaming, and wheat-laden ships bring him from Egypt over the flashing sea, wealth beyond count. Thus does the wine-drinker's heart leap with fancies.

BACCHYLIDES: *Fragment 27*
Greek lyric poet (5th century B.C.)

There is no gladness without wine.

BABYLONIAN TALMUD: *Pesachim*
(c. 5th century B.C.)

Wine is at the head of all medicines; where wine is lacking, drugs are necessary.

BABYLONIAN TALMUD: *Baba Bathra*

Wine will make a man intelligent.

BABYLONIAN TALMUD: *Joma*

Good wine's the gift that God has given
To man alone beneath the heaven,
Of dance and song the genial sire,
Of friendship gay and soft desire;
Yet rule it with a tightened rein,
Nor moderate wisdom's rules disdain;
For when unchecked there's nought runs faster—
A useful slave, but cruel master.

PANYASIS
Greek epic poet (5th century B.C.)

Wine moistens and tempers the spirits, and lulls the cares of the mind to rest. . . . It revives our joys, and is oil to the dying flame of life. If we drink temperately, and small draughts at a time, the wine distills into our lungs like sweetest morning dew. . . . It is then the wine commits no rape upon our reason, but pleasantly invites us to agreeable mirth.

SOCRATES
Greek philosopher (c. 469-399 B.C.)

Wine is a remedy for the moroseness of old age.

PLATO: *Laws*
Greek philosopher (c. 427-c. 347 B.C.)

What is better adapted than the festive use of wine in the first place to test and in the second place to train the character of a man, if care be taken in the use of it? What is there cheaper or more innocent?

PLATO

No thing more excellent nor more valuable than wine was ever granted mankind by God.
>PLATO

When a man drinks wine at dinner he begins to be better pleased with himself.
>PLATO

I like best the wine drunk at the cost to others.
>DIOGENES THE CYNIC
>Greek philosopher (412-323 B.C.)

Tell me, I pray thee, how you life define?
To drink full goblets of rich Chian wine.
>ANTIPHANES
>Greek playwright (c. 408-c. 334 B.C.)

When men drink, then they are rich and successful and win lawsuits and are happy and help their friends. Quickly, bring me a beaker of wine, so that I may whet my mind and say something clever.
>ARISTOPHANES: *The Knights*
>Greek comedic playwright (c. 448-c. 388 B.C.)

And when we pour libations
to the gods, we pour the god of wine himself
that through his intercession man may win
the favor of heaven.
>EURIPIDES: *The Bacchae*
>Greek playwright (480-406 B.C.)

Where there is no wine, love perishes, and everything else that is pleasant to man.
>EURIPIDES: *The Bacchae*

And so, my lord, whoever that power may be, receive him in our city, for he is great, in all these ways, and also, I hear tell, he gives to mortals the consoling vine; take wine away, and there will be no love, nor any other joy to mortals left.

EURIPIDES: *The Bacchae*

Equally blessing the rich, the poor, he has conferred the joy of wine.

EURIPIDES: *The Bacchae*

Mankind. . . possesses two supreme blessings. First of these is the goddess Demeter, or Earth—whichever name you choose to call her by. It was she who gave to man his nourishment of grain. But after her there came the son of Semele, who matched her present by inventing liquid wine as his gift to man. For filled with that good gift, suffering mankind forgets its grief; from it comes sleep; with it oblivion of the troubles of the day. There is no other medicine for misery.

EURIPIDES: *The Bacchae*

In Thasian wine or Chian soak your throttle,
Or take of Lesbian an old cobwebbed bottle.

EUBULUS: *Fragments*
Greek philosopher (4th century B.C.)

Man in no one respect resembles wine;
For man by age is made intolerable
But age improves all wine.

ALEXIS
Greek dramatist (4th and 3rd centuries B.C.)

There is no wine sweeter on the palate than Lesbian.

ALEXIS

This is the tomb of Callimachus that thou art passing. He could sing well, and laugh well at the right time over the wine.

> CALLIMACHUS: *his own epitaph*
> Alexandrian poet, grammarian, and critic
> (3rd century B.C.)

Go thy way, eat thy bread with joy, and drink thy wine with a merry heart; for God now accepteth thy works.

> ECCLESIASTES 9:7
> (c. 3rd century B.C.)

Give, in return for old wine, a new song.

> PLAUTUS: *Stichus*
> Roman comic poet (c. 250-184 B.C.)

Men should control the effects of wine, not wine men.

> PLAUTUS: *Truculentus*

Venus, of that I have, I'll give you a very, very little. I pour you a few drops as a libation. But they must be very, very few for I hate to spare them. After all, fair goddess, you get wine from all the lovers when they're drinking and want your favour. As for me, such gifts seldom come my way.

> PLAUTUS

Ah, the sweet, sweet smell of old wine, that meets my nostrils. It draws me into the open, dark as it is. I love it so. I need it so. Wherever is it? Ah, it's near, near.

Oh, joy! I have found it. Ah, there, sweetheart mine, beauty of Bacchus! You're old like me. The old will comfort the old. Why the odour of all the essences are only stinking water as compared with yours. You're my rose, my oil of cassia and saffron, my myrrh, my cinnamon.

> PLAUTUS

Without food and wine, love starves.
TERENTIUS: *Eunuchus*
Roman comic poet (c. 190-159 B.C.)

Wine was created from the beginning to make men joyful, and not to make them drunk.
ECCLESIASTICUS 5:35, *The Apocrypha*
(c. 2nd century B.C.)

Wine is like life to men, if you drink it in moderation. What is life to a man who is without wine? It has been created to make men glad.
ECCLESIASTICUS 31:27

Wine drunk in season and temperately
is rejoicing of heart and gladness of soul.
ECCLESIASTICUS 31:28

Wine new and old I drink,
of illness new and old I'm cured.
VARRO: *De Lingua Latina*
Roman scholar and writer (116-27 B.C.)

Bacchus loves the hillsides.
VIRGIL: *The Aeneid*
Latin poet (70-19 B.C.)

Nor our Italian vines produce the shape
Or taste or flavour of the Lesbian grape.
VIRGIL

The best wine for my beloved, that goeth down sweetly, causing the lips of those that are asleep to speak.
SONG OF SOLOMON 7:9

Drink, luckless lover! Thy heart's fiery rape,
Bacchus, who gives oblivion, shall assuage;
Drink deep; and while thou drain'st the brimming bowl,
Drive love's dark anguish from thy fevered soul.
>   MELEAGER
>   Palestinian epigrammist (1st century B.C.)

Let those who drink not, but austerely dine,
Dry up in law; the Muses smell of wine.
>   HORACE
>   Roman poet and satirist (65-8 B.C.)

Why not at ease beneath this pine
Our whitening hair with roses twine,
And quaff the rich Falernian wine?
>   HORACE

Drink, comrades, drink; give loose to mirth!
With joyous footstep beat the earth,
And spread before the War-God's shrine
The Salian feast, the sacrificial wine.
>   HORACE

Slaves! the beaker fill once more
>   With potent draughts of Massic wine!
Forth from shells capacious pour
>   Indian essences divine.
>   HORACE

>   Haste;
A cask unbroached of mellow wine
Awaits thee, roses interlaced,
And perfumes pressed from nard divine.
>   HORACE

Drinking with purpled lip the nectar of the gods.
HORACE

Come, Thaliarchus, now dispel the cold,
Spare not the faggots, make a roaring fire,
Bring out the jar of Sabine four-year-old,
Let plenteous draughts of wine good cheer inspire.
HORACE

Bacchus drowns within the bowl
Troubles that corrode the soul.
HORACE

Wine is mighty to inspire new hopes and wash away the bitters of care.
HORACE: *Carmina*

What miracle cannot the wine-cup work? It lifts the load from anxious hearts.
HORACE: *Epistles*

What tongue hangs fire when quickened by the bowl?
What wretch so poor but wine expands his soul?
HORACE: *Epistles*

What cannot wine perform? It brings to light
The secret soul, it bids the coward fight:
Gives being to our hopes, and from our hearts
Drives the dull sorrow, and inspires new arts.
Is there a wretch whom bumpers have not taught
A flow of words and loftiness of thought?
Even in the oppressive grasp of poverty
It can enlarge and bid the soul be free.
HORACE: *Epistles*

No poems can live long or please that are written by water-drinkers.

HORACE: *Odes*

Who, after wine, talks of war's hardships or of poverty?

HORACE: *Odes*

Smooth out with wine the worries of a wrinkled brow.

HORACE: *Satires*

Bacchus opens the gates of the heart.

HORACE: *Satires*

See me, mighty Bacchus, prone at your altar, a lowly supplicant for your help. O father grant me peace and prosper my petition. I am a grave offender against Venus but thou canst pacify her anger, and troubles find balm from thy Wine. . . . O Bacchus wash my heart clean from this weakness. . . . Only death or thy wine can drive from my body this torment that for many years has blazed with unholy fury. But if by virtue of thy gifts, O father, thou bringst sleep to rest my weary eyes and soul, then will I plant vines in rows upon my hills in thine honor, and will bid my servant watch that no savage beast dishonor them.

If only I may fill my vats to overflowing with purple must, and the juice may dye the feet which tread the wine-press, then as long as life lasts, thou and thy horns shall bring my inspiration, and I, O Bacchus, will be thy poet for ever-more. . . . Outside the gates of your temple shall rest the bowl, filled with Wine, and the priest shall dip with golden ladle the precious liquid and pour it on the sacrifice to thine honor. . . . O father, hear my prayer, save me from this pitiless tyranny, and soothe an anguished brain with gentle sleep.

PROPERTIUS
Roman elegiac poet (c.48-c. 15 B.C.)

Let wine crushed in Falernian presses flow freely. Let the poet, inspired by wine, call upon his muse for songs of joy and laughter. Bacchus 'tis thy pleasure to hold the hours of darkness for the coming of Apollo. Thus will I pass the night with drink and good cheer 'till dawn cast golden bars across the purple of my wine.

> PROPERTIUS

Wine timely given aids untimely opportunites.

> PROPERTIUS

Away with you, Water, destruction of wine.

> CATULLUS: *Odes*
> Roman lyric poet (c. 84-c. 54 B.C.)

Was it not the skillful hand of Osiris that indicated how to join the young vine to the pole, how to lop the green leaves with the grim hook of the pruner? For him the ripe grapes, crushed by trampling feet, first yielded up their agreeable flavour. Their juice taught men to attune the voice to mirth and sorrow, and told unaccustomed limbs to move in gracious harmony. When the heart of the peasant is crushed with arduous labour, it is Bacchus who draws it back to joyfulness, loosens it from the bands of sorrow. To mortals wrapt in distress, the Wine-god brings relief, even though the hated gyves encompass their legs.

> TIBULLUS
> Roman elegiac poet (c. 30 B.C.)

When there is plenty of wine, sorrow and worry take wing.

> OVID: *The Art of Love*
> Latin poet (43 B.C.-17 A.D.)

Wine prepares the heart for love,
Unless you take too much.

> OVID: *The Art of Love*

Wine rouses the heart, inclines to passion: Heavy drinking dilutes and banishes care in a sea of laughter, gives the poor man self-confidence, smooths out wrinkles, puts paid to pain and sorrow.

OVID: *The Art of Love*

Wine over dinner was rather meant to promote fun and games.

OVID: *The Art of Love*

It warms the blood, adds luster to the eyes,
And wine and love have ever been allies.

OVID: *The Art of Love*

For the hasty, new-bottled wine; for me, a vintage laid down long years before.

OVID: *The Art of Love*

You get the best vintage from well-cared-for grapes.

OVID: *The Art of Love*

Bacchus too helps lovers, fosters that flame with which he burns himself.

OVID: *The Art of Love*

This festive day calls for wine, for love-making and song—what fitter tribute to all-powerful gods.

OVID: *The Amores*

Then let us quaff it, let us everywhere
E'er joy and mirth combine!
And if we knew a man bow'd by despair,
We'd give to him the wine.

CLAUDIUS
Roman emperor (10 B.C.-54 A.D.)

The best kind of wine is that which is most pleasant to him who drinks it.

> PLINY THE ELDER: *Natural History*
> Roman author and viticulturalist (23-79 A.D.)

It has become quite a common proverb that in wine there is truth. (In vino veritas.)

> PLINY THE ELDER: *Natural History*

Nothing is more useful than wine for strengthening the body and also more detrimental to our pleasures if moderation be lacking.

> PLINY THE ELDER: *Natural History*

Wine has the property of heating the parts of the body inside when it is drunk and of cooling them when poured on the outside.

> PLINY THE ELDER: *Natural History*

Wine nourishes the strength, blood, and complexion of men. It distinguishes the middle and temperate zone from those on either side of it. We gain such vigor from the juice of the grape as others gain from the extremes of their climates. Wine refreshes the stomach, sharpens the appetite, blunts care and sadness, and woos over sleep.

> PLINY THE ELDER: *Natural History*

Drink no longer water, but use a little wine for thy stomach's sake and thine often infirmities.

> I TIMOTHY 5:23, *New Testament*
> (c. 50-97 A.D.)

This cup is the new testament in my blood: this do ye, as oft as ye drink it, in remembrance of me.

> I CORINTHIANS 11:25, *New Testament*
> (c. 52-55 A.D.)

And he took the cup, and when he had given thanks, he gave it to them: and they all drank of it. And he said unto them, This is my blood of the new testament, which is shed for many.

> MARK 14:23-24, *New Testament*
> (c. 65-70 A.D.)

Neither do men put new wine into old bottles: else the bottles break, and the wine runneth out, and the bottles perish: but they put new wine into new bottles, and both are preserved.

> MATTHEW 9:17, *New Testament*
> (c. 80 A.D.)

But I say unto you, I will not drink henceforth of this fruit of the vine until that day when I drink it new with you in my Father's kingdom.

> MATTHEW 26:29

No man also having drunk old wine straightway desireth new: for he saith, the old is better.

> LUKE 5:39, *New Testament*
> (c. 80 A.D.)

A person warmed with wine will never either teach, or be convinced by, one who is sober.

> EPICTETUS: *Encheiridion*
> Roman philosopher (1st century A.D.)

Wine is life.
> PETRONIUS
> Roman satirist (1st century A.D.)

You will make the wine good by drinking it.
> MARTIAL: *Epigrams*
> Roman poet and epigrammist (c. 40-c. 104 A.D.)

Never think of giving perfumes or wine to your heir. Let him have your money, but give these to yourself.
> MARTIAL: *Epigrams*

A jar of wine so priceless did not deserve to die.
> MARTIAL

Wine not only strengthens the natural heat but also clarifies turbid blood and opens the passages of the whole body. It strengthens also the members. And its goodness is not only revealed in the body but also in the soul, for it makes the soul merry and lets it forget sadness.
> RUFUS OF EPHESUS
> Greek anatomist and physician (98-117 A.D.)

Every man at the beginning doth set forth good wine; and when men have well drunk, then that which is worse: but thou hast kept the good wine until now.
> JOHN 2:10
> (c. 100 A.D.)

Toward evening, about suppertime, when the serious studies of the day are over, is the time to take wine.
> CLEMENT OF ALEXANDRIA: *Paedagogus*
> Greek philosopher and church father (c. 150-c. 215 A.D.)

[Wine] makes the eyes quick to see, turns all things fairer and brings back the blessings of fair youth.

> GAIUS MAECENAS
> Roman jurist (130-180 A.D.)

Among the Egyptians of ancient times, any kind of gathering was conducted with moderation. . . . They dined while seated using the simplest and most healthful food and only as much wine as would be sufficient to promote good cheer.

> ATHENAEUS: *Deipnosophistai*
> Greek writer and grammarian (3rd century A.D.)

Wine seems to have the power of attracting friendship, warming and fusing hearts together.

> ATHENAEUS: *Deipnosophistai*

I hear many cry when deplorable excesses happen, "Would there were no wine!" Oh, folly! oh, madness! Is it the wine that causes this abuse? No. It is the intemperance of those who take an evil delight in it. Cry rather: "Would to God there were no drunkenness, no luxury." If you say, "Would there were no wine" because of the drunkards, then you must say, going on by degrees, "Would there were no steel" because of the murderers, "Would there were no night" because of the thieves, "Would there were no light" because of the informers, and "Would there were no women" because of adultery.

> ST. JOHN CHRYSOSTOM: *Homilies*
> Religious scholar (c. 347-407)

Wine was given by God, not that we might be drunken, but that we might be sober. It is the best medicine when it has the moderation to direct it. Wine was given to restore the body's weakness, not to overturn the soul's strength.

> ST. JOHN CHRYSOSTOM: *Homilies*

O~LD~ F~RIENDS~ K~NOW~ W~HAT~ I L~IKE~

Old friends know what I like:
They bring wine whenever they come by.
We spread out and sit under the pines;
After several rounds, we're drunk again.
Old men chatting away—all at once;
Passing the jug around—out of turn.
Unaware that there is a "self",
How do we learn to value "things"?
We are lost in these deep thoughts;
In wine, there is a heady taste.

> T'AO CHI'EN
> Chinese poet (c. 372-427)

Then let the goblet gleam for me, my friend;
Pour forth care-soothing wine ere pleasures end.

> PALLADAS
> Greek epigrammist (5th century A.D.)

What is stronger than wine foaming in the press?

> AHIKAR: *Teachings*
> Egyptian philosopher (5th century A.D.)

WINE
IN THE
MIDDLE
AGES

(c. 475 - c. 1450)

RELIGION PLAYED A PROMINENT ROLE in shaping the history of wine during the Middle Ages. The Christian church was the single most significant factor in the proliferation of the grapevine and the development of wine. As Christianity spread so did viticulture and winemaking, via the monasteries. In fact, many of present-day Europe's finest vineyards were established centuries ago by various religious sects.

The monasteries not only increased the supply of wine available to the public, they conducted research and developed techniques which led to the overall improvement of wine. As the beverage became more refined and available, its popularity soared. Wine trading soon became a big commerce throughout Europe.

The majority of wines produced during this era were reds, largely because they were more aesthetically appealing in religious ceremonies where wine was symbolic of Christ's blood. When the Catholic Church established a papal seat in Avignon, France, the Chateauneuf-du-Pape wines were developed, and the concept of "cru" designation came into effect in France.

The biggest impact upon the European wine world, however, occurred in 1152 when Eleanor of Aquitane married Henri Plantagenet. When Henri became King Henry II of England, all of his wife's possessions in France became his, including the great wine-producing region of Bordeaux. For the next three hundred years the merchants of Bordeaux were able to sell their wines as Englishmen rather than as foreigners, thus avoiding significant taxes and ensuring the popularity of Bordeaux wines in England for many generations.

Unfortunately, wine did not fare as well in other parts of the world during this time. During the reign of Mohammed in the late sixth and early seventh centuries, wine was outlawed by Islamic law in the Arab culture, although it had been used extensively by that civilization for hundreds of years.

While the Middle Ages were a rather bleak period of history in most aspects, they were a favorable chapter as far as wine was concerned. The emphasis which the church placed upon the production of wine and the extension of viticulture guaranteed wine a place of prominence which was to endure for many centuries to come.

Drinking Alone in the Moonlight

If Heaven did not love wine,
There would be no Wine Star in Heaven.
If Earth did not love wine,
There should be no Wine Springs on Earth.
Why then be ashamed before Heaven to love wine.
I have heard that clear wine is like the Sages;
Again it is said that thick wine is like the Virtuous Worthies.
Wherefore it appears that we have swallowed both Sages and
    Worthies.
Why should we strive to be Gods and Immortals?
Three cups, and one can perfectly understand the Great Tao;
A gallon, and one is in accord with all nature.
Only those in the midst of it can fully comprehend the joys of
    wine;
I do not proclaim them to the sober.

      Li Po
      Chinese poet (c. 700-762)

What is this life you are so sure about?
A flame that kindles, flashes, and goes out,
The unchanging heaven and the eternal sea
Serve but to mock our mutability.
And you before this wine who hesitate
For what, I ask you frankly, do you wait?

      Li Po

Riches and poverty, long or short life,
By the maker of things are proportioned and disposed;
But a cup of wine levels life and death
And a thousand things obstinately hard to prove.

      Li Po: *Fragments*

The rapture of drinking
And wine's dizzy joy
No man who is sober deserves.

      Li Po: *Fragments*

Secure the heights and set a vineyard where the ground is clear.

> CHARLEMAGNE
> King of the Franks and Roman emperor (742-814)

How great a thing is a single cup of wine!
For it makes us tell the story of our whole lives.

> PO CHU-I
> Chinese poet (772-846)

BETTER COME DRINK WINE WITH ME

Don't go hide in the deep mountains—
you'll only come to hate it.
Your teeth will ache with the chill of dawn water,
your face smart from the bite of the night frost.
Go off fishing and winds will blow up from the cove;
return from gathering firewood to find snow all over the cliffs.
Better come drink wine with me;
face to face we'll get mellowly, mellowly drunk.

Don't go off and be a farmer—
you'll only make yourself miserable.
Come spring and you'll be plowing the lean soil,
twilight and it's time to feed the skinny ox.
Again and again you'll be hit for government taxes,
but seldom will you meet up with a year of good crops.
Better come drink wine with me;
together we'll get quietly, quietly drunk.

Don't go climbing up to the blue clouds—
the blue clouds are rife with passion and hate,
everyone a wise man, bragging of knowledge and vision,
flattening each other in the scramble for merit and power.
Fish get chowdered because they swallow the bait;
moths burn up when they bumble into the lamp.
Better come drink wine with me;
let yourself go, get roaring, roaring drunk.

Don't go into the realm of red dust—
it wears out a person's spirit and strength.
You war with each other like the two horns of a snail,
end up with one ox-hair worth of gain.
Put out the fire that burns in your rage,
stop whetting the knife that hides in a smile.
Better come drink wine with me;
we'll lie down peacefully, merrily, merrily drunk.

      Po Chu-I

If a problem was too difficult for me, I returned to the Mosque and prayed, invoking the Creator of all things until the gate that had been closed to me was opened and what had been complex became simple. Always, as night fell, I returned to my house, set the lamp before me and busied myself with reading and writing. If sleep overcame me or I felt the flesh growing weak, I had recourse to a beaker of wine, so my energies were restored.

      Avicenna
      Arab physician and philosopher (980-1037)

Wine is also a beauty spot on the cheek of intelligence.

      Omar Khayyam: *The Rubaiyat*
      Persian poet and astronomer (c. 1048-1122)

How long, how long, in infinite Pursuit
Of This and That endeavor and dispute?
    Better be merry with the fruitful Grape
Than sadden after none, or bitter, Fruit.

      Omar Khayyam: *The Rubaiyat*

And lately, by the Tavern Door agape,
Came stealing through the Dusk an Angel Shape
    Bearing a Vessel on his Shoulder; and
He bid me taste of it; and 'twas—the Grape!

      Omar Khayyam: *The Rubaiyat*

The Grape that can with Logic absolute
The Two-and-Seventy jarring Sects confute;
     The subtle alchemist that in a Trice
Life's leaden Metal into Gold transmute.
     OMAR KHAYYAM: *The Rubaiyat*

Ah, with the Grape my fading Life provide,
And wash my Body whence the Life has died,
     And in a Winding-sheet of Vine-leaf wrapt,
So bury me by some sweet Garden-side.
     OMAR KHAYYAM: *The Rubaiyat*

A Book of Verses underneath the Bough,
A Jug of Wine, a Loaf of Bread—and Thou
     Beside me singing in the Wilderness—
Oh, Wilderness were Paradise enow.
     OMAR KHAYYAM: *The Rubaiyat*

And if the Wine you drink, the Lip you press,
End in what All begins and ends in—Yes;
     Think then you are Today what Yesterday
You were—Tomorrow you shall not be less.
     OMAR KHAYYAM: *The Rubaiyat*

You know, my Friends, with what a brave Carouse
I made a Second Marriage in my house;
     Divorced old barren Reason from my Bed,
And took the Daughter of the Vine to Spouse.
     OMAR KHAYYAM: *The Rubaiyat*

Comrades, I pray you, physic me with wine
Make this wan amber face like rubies shine
     And if I die, use wine to wash my corpse
And lay me in a coffin made of vine.
     OMAR KHAYYAM: *The Rubaiyat*

The Wine of Life keeps oozing drop by drop,
The Leaves of Life keep falling one by one.
>   OMAR KHAYYAM: *The Rubaiyat*

Now of old joys nought but the name is left
Of all old friends but wine we are bereft
>   And that wine new; but still cleave to the cup
For save the cup what solace is there left.
>   OMAR KHAYYAM: *The Rubaiyat*

I wonder often what the Vintners buy
One half so precious as the Goods they sell.
>   OMAR KHAYYAM: *The Rubaiyat*

But still the vine her ancient Ruby yields.
>   OMAR KHAYYAM: *The Rubaiyat*

The benefits of wine are many if it is taken in the proper amount, as it keeps the body in a healthy condition and cures many illnesses. But knowledge of its consumption is hidden from the masses.
>   MAIMONIDES: *De Regimine Sanitatis*
>   Jewish philosopher and physician (1135-1204)

I intend to die in a tavern; let the wine be placed near my dying mouth, so that when the choirs of angels come, they may say, "God be merciful to this drinker!"
>   WALTER MAPES: *De Nugis Curialium*
>   Welsh poet and ecclesiastic (c. 1137-1209)

If a man deliberately abstains from wine to such an extent that he does serious harm to his nature, he will not be free from blame.
>   SAINT THOMAS AQUINAS
>   Italian scholar and theologian (1225-1274)

If wine is taken in the right measure it suits every age, every time and every region. It is becoming to the old because it opposes their dryness. To the young it is a food, because the nature of wine is the same as that of young people. But to children it is also a food because it increases their natural heat.

ARNALDUS: *Liber de Vinis*
Greek physician (c. 1235-1311)

Hence it comes that men experienced in the art of healing have chosen the wine and have written many chapters about it and have declared it to be a useful embodiment or combination of all things for common usage. It truly is most friendly to human nature.

ARNALDUS: *Liber de Vinis*

And that you may the less marvel at my words,
Look at the sun's heat that becomes the wine
When combined with the juice that flows from the vine.

DANTE
Italian poet and philosopher (1265-1321)

On a moonlit night, a morning after a snowfall, or under the cherry blossoms, it adds to our pleasure if, while chatting at our ease, we bring forth the wine cups. Liquor is cheering on days when we are bored, or when a friend pays an unexpected visit. It is exceedingly agreeable too when you are offered cakes and wine most elegantly from behind a screen of state by a person of quality you do not know especially well. In winter it is delightful to sit opposite an intimate friend in a small room, toasting something to eat over the fire, and to drink deeply together.

YOSHIDA KENKO: *Essays in Idleness*
Japanese philosopher (c. 1282-1350)

One should write not unskillfully in the running hand, be able to sing in a pleasing voice and keep good time to music; and, lastly, a man should not refuse a little wine when pressed upon him.

> YOSHIDA KENKO: *Essays in Idleness*

the whole grove, red leaves flutter in confusion
drunk through autumn frost as bright trees are ravished
quietly brush off the green moss and sit there writing poems
the wine is warm
      if the brazier's cold
the cup is deep
and wine can wash away the pain of autumn
I loosen my robe, leave things alone
drink the bowl dry.

> KUAN YUN-SHIH: *Knowing Enough IV*
> Chinese poet (1286-1324)

Wine is wholesome, gives health to the sick, joy to the sorrowful, courage and bravery to those who are well.

> BRIDGET OF SWEDEN: *Revelations*
> Swedish visionary (c. 1302-73)

The roses have come, nor can anything afford so much pleasure as a goblet of wine.

> HAFIZ: *Odes*
> Persian historian and lyrical poet (c. 1324-1391)

Give me wine! Wine shall subdue the strongest; that I may for a time forget the cares and troubles of this world.

> HAFIZ: *Odes*

The only friends who are free from care are the goblet of wine and a book of odes.

> HAFIZ: *Odes*

A book of verses and a cup of pure wine,
Are truly your most intimate friends.
Watch your road for it has curves and bends;
Enjoy wine for only once is life thine.

> HAFIZ: *Odes*

WINE WORSHIP

Saki, the dawn is breaking;
    Fill up the glass with wine.
Heaven's wheel no delay is making—
    Haste, haste, while the day is thine!

Ere to our final ruin
    Space and the world speed by,
Let wine be our great undoing,
    Red wine, let us drink and die!

See, on the bowl's horizon
    Wine, the red sun, doth rise:
Here's glory to feast the eyes on—
    Drive sleep from thy languid eyes!

When Fate on his wheel is moulding
    Jars from this clay of mine,
Let this be the cup thou'rt holding
    And fill up my head with wine!

Never was I a shrinker,
    No hypocrite monk am I;
Let wine, the pure wine of the drinker
    Be the talk men address me by.

Wine is the sole salvation,
    Its worship and works sublime;
Be firm thy determination,
    Hafiz—be saved in time!

> HAFIZ

On turnpikes of wonder wine leads the mind forth.
    HAFIZ: *Odes*

To the wise comes there a cup, fired of the night,
    pressed to the lip;
And he bow not to the Wine Creed, be he writ Love's renegade.
    HAFIZ: *Wild of Mien*

All my pleasure is to sip
Wine from my beloved's lip;
I have gained the utmost bliss—
God alone be praised for this.
    HAFIZ: *All My Pleasure*

The house of hope is built on sand,
    And life's foundations rest on air;
Then come, give wine into my hand,
That we may make an end of care.
    HAFIZ: *The House of Hope*

He seyde: "I see well it is necessarie,
Where that we goon, good wyn with us carie
For that wol turne rancour and disese
T'accord and love, and many a wrong apese."
    GEOFFREY CHAUCER: *The Canterbury Tales*
    English poet (c. 1345-1400)

After wyn, on Venus moste I thinke.
    GEOFFREY CHAUCER: *Wife of Bath's Prologue*

72

WINE DURING THE RENAISSANCE

(c. 1450 - c. 1660)

DURING THE RENAISSANCE, art, literature, architecture, and learning all flourished. So, too, did wine. Europe was a well-established wine-growing region by the mid-fifteenth century, and wine was the beverage of choice in everyday life for all but the very poorest of the population. Consumed at mealtimes, as well as during leisure hours, it was considered an essential part of the diet. The water of Renaissance Europe was polluted and unsafe to drink; wine and beer were the only alternatives.

In 1453, after the Battle of Castillon, the Bordeaux region reverted to France, having spent the previous three hundred years as a property of England. As a result, the English trade in French wines suffered a serious setback. Although the Bordeaux wines continued to be in high demand in England, they developed greater competition in the market as the wine trade opened up with other countries.

England witnessed the rise in popularity of a great many foreign wines, and by the sixteenth century such favorites included sherry (commonly called sack) from Spain, madeira (also known as malmsey and malvasia) from the Portuguese island of Madeira, and rhenish wines from Germany. In fact, German wines were at the forefront of many foreign markets during this time.

The majority of wine during the Renaissance period was consumed at a young age. It was in great demand and it was cheap. Since the wine trade of England constituted an important commodity of the country's economy, wine was strictly controlled. The general populace was not allowed to keep wine in its homes—only vintners, licensed taverns, and selected nobility were able to possess the sacred beverage. This was the reason for the profusion of taverns throughout England. Everyone drank wine as a daily beverage, but ordinary people couldn't have it in their homes, so they spent much of their time frequenting the local taverns, inns, and public houses.

A sense of camaraderie developed within these watering holes as people met regularly at the end of the day to relax, eat, drink, and, most importantly, converse. Politics, religion, commerce, art, literature, and philosophy were all discussed over a glass of wine—this was the era of conversation as a true art form, a stimulation of the mind. Wine enhanced the exchange of ideas and the flow of conversation. As a result, more wine was imported into England during this period than during the present day, despite the obvious difference in population.

The advent of the sixteenth century had also witnessed the discovery of the New World. The early explorers of the eastern North American continent discovered an abundant growth of wild grapevines, but after establishing several settlements, soon discovered that the particular species (*vitis labrusca*) which flourished there was not conducive to making quality European-style wines. And, since very few wines of the time were able to survive the long ocean voyages, cuttings of vines were brought along as early as 1616 to establish vineyards. Wine was still used as a daily beverage, and the early colonists, therefore, considered it a necessary component of life.

Unfortunately, the European variety of grapevine, *vitis vinifera*, was unable to withstand the harsh climate of the New World, and the vines which were planted either died or failed to produce fruit. Beer and cider, which could easily be produced, were used as alternatives.

In Europe, the seventeenth century brought about a great many changes which had a substantial negative impact upon wine. Distilled spirits were introduced and gave wine some stiff competition. In addition, beer became more fashionable (and of better quality), tobacco had been introduced and soon supplanted both beer and wine, and an aqueduct into London brought in water which was safe to consume.

If that weren't enough for wine to endure, coffee soon came into vogue, and coffee houses appeared throughout London, taking the places of the local taverns. Tea was soon to follow. Suddenly, England had a wealth of beverages from which to choose, and wine's popularity suffered. In Germany, beer became the national drink, replacing wine. And, the colonists of the New World discovered that the distilled spirits had no problem surviving the treacherous ocean voyages; rum soon became a popular beverage here.

Fortunately, the seventeenth century as a whole was not an entirely negative period for wine in Europe. During this time the procedure for producing champagne was developed by Dom Perignon in France. In addition, as the French nobility entered the wine trade, higher standards of winemaking produced better wines because these wealthy landowners could afford to be exacting and demanding in the quality of the finished beverage.

Also during this period bottles and corks began to be used for storing wines. Although the ancient Romans had used corks, their usage had been lost through the ages. Up until then, cloth, leather, straw, and other such items had been tried with very little success. The corks offered an opportunity for wine to be stored for extended periods of time, and, thus, develop into better quality wines as they underwent the aging process.

So, in spite of the adverse competition which wine received from beer, distilled spirits, coffee, tea, and even tobacco during the middle of the Renaissance, this period also witnessed a flourishing of wine at its beginning and a potential for enhanced and continued greatness at its end. The history of wine was to become vintage once again.

Wine, the Pegasus of poets.
>PONTANUS: *Collectio Proverbiorum*
>Italian poet and statesman (1426-1503)

I feast on wine and bread, and feasts they are.
>MICHELANGELO
>Italian painter, sculptor, and poet (1475-1564)

Beer is made by men, wine by God!
>MARTIN LUTHER
>German scholar and reformer (1483-1546)

Choose your wine after this sort; it must be fragrant and redolent, having a good odour and flavour in the nose; it must sprinkle in the cup when it is drawn or put out of the pot into the cup; it must be cold and pleasant in the mouth; and it must be strong and subtle of substance. And then moderately drunken it doth quicken a man's wits, it doth comfort the heart, it doth scour the liver; specially, if it be white wine, it doth rejoice all the powers of man, and doth nourish them; it doth engender good blood, it doth comfort and doth nourish the brain and all the body, and it resolveth fleume; it engendereth heat, and it is good against heaviness and pensifulness; it is full of agility; wherefore it is medicinable, specially white wine, for it doth mundify and cleanse wounds and sores.
>ANDREW BOORDE: *A Dyetary of Helth*
>English physician (c. 1490-1549)

I drink eternally. This is to me an eternity of drinking and drinking of eternity. . . . I moisten my windpipe with wine— I drink to banish all fear of dying—Drink but deep enough and you shall live forever. If the parchment on which is endorsed my bonds and bills could drink as well as I, my creditors would never need to buy wine when I settle my just dues.
>FRANCOIS RABELAIS: *Life of Gargantua and Pantagruel*
>French author, monk, and doctor (c. 1494-1553)

Never did a man of good worth dislike good wine, it is a monastical apophthegm.

FRANCOIS RABELAIS: *Gargantua*

O the fine white wine, upon my soul it is a kind of taffetas wine.

FRANCOIS RABELAIS: *Gargantua*

Bottle! whose Mysterious Deep
Do's ten thousand secrets keep,
With attentive ear I wait;
Ease my mind and speak my Fate.
Soul of joy! Like Bacchus, we
More than India gain by thee.
Truths unborn thy Juice reveals
Which futurity conceals.
Antidote to Frauds and Lyes,
Wine that mounts us to the skies,
May thy Father Noah's brood
Like him drown, but in thy Blood.
Speak, so may the liquid Mine
Of Rubies, or of Diamonds, shine,
Bottle! whose Mysterious Deep,
Do's ten thousand secrets keep,
With attentive ear I wait,
Ease my mind and speak my Fate.

FRANCOIS RABELAIS: *The Temple of Bacchus*

And here we maintain that not laughter but drinking is proper to man. I don't mean simple, unadorned drinking because the beasts drink as well. I mean drinking good cool wine. Note well, my friends, that through wine one becomes divine.

FRANCOIS RABELAIS: *Cinquiesme Livre*

79

Some use wine for profit, some to make them merry withal, and some for pleasure, and some for all these purposes. Wine doth not only nourish, but maketh the meats to go well down, and stirreth up the natural heat and increaseth it. . . . But if a man will use it wisely, it will digest or distribute the nourishment, increase the blood and nourish; it will also make the mind both gentler and bolder.

> WILLIAM TURNER, M.D.: *New Book . . . of all Wines*
> English clergyman, physician, and botanist (1510-68)

Now good reader, seeing that almighty God our heavenly father hath given thee this noble creature of wine, so manye wayes profitable to our bodies and mindes, thanke him with all thy heart, not onely for it, but also for that he hath sent learned Physitians to tell thee how, in what measure, and in what time thou should use them.

> WILLIAM TURNER, M.D.: *New Book . . . of all Wines*

And in the wine a solemn oth they bynd.

> EDMUND SPENSER: *The Faerie Queen*
> English poet (1522-99)

After bread comes wine, the second nutriment given by the Creator to sustain life and the first to be famed for its excellence.

> OLIVIER DE SERRES: *Theatre de l'Agriculture*
> French agronomist (1539-1619)

After hee hath well mingled water in his wyne, hee may chaunce to finde cause of repentance.

> WILLIAM PAINTER: *The Pallace of Pleasure*
> English translator (c. 1540-94)

Where wine is not common, commons must be sent.

> WILLIAM CAMDEN: *Remains*
> English scholar and historian (1551-1623)

As Plinie saith, wine so it be moderately vsed, is a thing ordeined of god. It doth quench the thirst, reuiue the spirites, comfort the hart, sharpen the wyt, gladdeth a doleful mind, maketh a good memorye, killeth yl humors, maketh good blood.

> JOHN FLORIO: *Firste Fruites*
> English scholar (c. 1553-1625)

Th' water hurteth, wyne maketh one sing.

> JOHN FLORIO: *Firste Fruites*

Water and wine is good against the heat of the liver.

> ROBERT GREENE: *A Quip for an Upstart Courtier*
> English dramatist (1558-92)

Choose wine you mean shall serve you all the year,
Well-favoured, tasting well, and coloured clear.
Five qualities there are wine's praise advancing:
Strong, beautiful, fragrant, cool, and dancing.

> JOHN HARINGTON: *The Englishman's Doctor*
> English writer and courtier (1561-1612)

And overhead
A lively vine of sea-green agates pread,
Where by one hand light-headed Bacchus hung,
And with the other wine from grapes outwrung.

> CHRISTOPHER MARLOWE
> English dramatist and poet (1562-1593)

Give me a bowl of wine.
I have not that alacrity of spirit
Nor cheer of mind that I was wont to have.

> WILLIAM SHAKESPEARE: *Richard III*
> English dramatist and poet (1564-1616)

Come and crush a cup of wine.
WILLIAM SHAKESPEARE: *Romeo and Juliet*

With mirth and laughter let old wrinkles come,
And let my liver rather heat with wine
Than my heart cool with mortifying groans.
WILLIAM SHAKESPEARE: *The Merchant of Venice*

A cup of wine that's brisk and fine,
And drink unto the leman mine;
And a merry heart lives long-a.
Fill the cup and let it come,
I'll pledge you a mile to the bottom.
WILLIAM SHAKESPEARE: *Henry IV*

A good sherris-sack hath a two-fold operation in it. It ascends me into the brain; dries me there all the foolish and dull and crudy vapours which environ it; makes it apprehensive, quick, forgetive, full of nimble, fiery, and delectable shapes; which, delivered o'er to the voice, the tongue, which is the birth, becomes excellent wit. The second property of your excellent sherris is, the warming of the blood; which, before cold and settled, left the liver white and pale, which is the badge of pusillanimity and cowardice; but the sherris warms it and makes it course from the inwards to the parts extremes. It illumineth the face, which as a beacon gives warning to all the rest of this little kingdom, man, to arm; and then the vital commoners and inland petty spirits muster me all to their captain, the heart, who, great and puff'd up with this retinue, doth any deed of courage; and this valour comes of sherris. So that skill in the weapon is nothing without sack, for that sets it a-work; and learning a mere hoard of gold kept by a devil, till sack commences it and set it in act and use.
WILLIAM SHAKESPEARE: *Henry IV*

Nor a man cannot make him laugh; but that is no marvel, he drinks no wine.

WILLIAM SHAKESPEARE: *Henry IV*

Fill what you will, and drink what you fill.
Go fetch me a quart of sack, put a toast in't.

WILLIAM SHAKESPEARE: *The Merry Wives of Windsor*

Good friends, go in and taste some wine with me;
And we like friends will straightway go together.

WILLIAM SHAKESPEARE: *Julius Caesar*

Give me a bowl of wine.
In this I bury all unkindness.

WILLIAM SHAKESPEARE: *Julius Caesar*

Good wine needs no bush.

WILLIAM SHAKESPEARE: *As You Like It*

Good wine is a good familiar creature, if it be
well us'd; exclaim no more against it.

WILLIAM SHAKESPEARE: *Othello*

Come, love and health to all:
Then I'll sit down. Give me some wine, fill full,
I drink to the general joy
o' the whole table.

WILLIAM SHAKESPEARE: *MacBeth*

There's nothing serious in mortality.
All is but toys; renown and grace is dead,
The wine of life is drawn, and the mere lees
Is left this vault to brag of.

WILLIAM SHAKESPEARE: *MacBeth*

Come, thou monarch of the vine,
Plumpy Bacchus with pink eyne!
In thy fats our cares be drown'd,
With thy grapes our hairs be crown'd!
Cup us, till the world go round,
Cup us, till the world go round!
    WILLIAM SHAKESPEARE: *Antony and Cleopatra*

Come, let's all take hands,
Till that the conquering wine hath steep'd our sense
In soft and delicate Lethe.
    WILLIAM SHAKESPEARE: *Antony and Cleopatra*

I am dying, Egypt, dying,
Give me some wine, and let me speak a little.
    WILLIAM SHAKESPEARE: *Antony and Cleopatra*

I am known to be. . . one that loves a cup of hot wine with not
a drop of allaying Tiber in't.
    WILLIAM SHAKESPEARE: *Coriolanus*

Good company, good wine, good welcome, make good
people.
    WILLIAM SHAKESPEARE: *Henry VIII*

The wine-cup is the little silver well
Where truth, if truth there be, doth dwell.
    WILLIAM SHAKESPEARE

To wine; kings it makes gods, and
Meaner creatures, kings.
    WILLIAM SHAKESPEARE

Wine is light, held together by water.

GALILEO
Italian astronomer and physicist (1564-1642)

Wine is a charm, it heats the blood too,
Cowards it will arm, if the wine be good too,
Quickens the wit and makes the back able,
Scorns to submit to the watch or constable.

THOMAS DEKKER
English playwright (c. 1572- c. 1632)

Welcome all, who lead or follow,
To the oracle of Apollo:
Here he speaks out of his pottle,
Or the tripos, his Tower bottle;
All his answers are divine—
Truth itself doth flow in wine.
'Hang up all the poor hop-drinkers,'
Cries old Sim, the king of skinkers.
He the half of life abuses
That sits watering with the muses.
Those dull girls no good can mean us;
Wine—it is the milk of Venus,
And the poet's horse accounted:
Ply it, and you all are mounted.
'Tis the true Phoebian liquor,
Cheers the brain, makes wit the quicker,
Pays all debts, cures all diseases,
And at once three senses pleases.
Welcome all, who lead or follow,
To the oracle of Apollo.

BEN JONSON: *Lines over the door of the Apollo Room of the old
Devil Tavern, Fleet Street, London*
English dramatist (1572-1637)

Swell me a bowl with lusty wine,
Till I may see the plump Lyaeus swim
　　Above the brim:
I drink as I would write,
In flowing measure fill'd with flame and sprite.
　　　　BEN JONSON: *The Poetaster*

Tonight grave sir, both my poor house and I
Do equally desire your company. . .

Digestive cheese and fruit there sure will be
But that which most doth take my muse and me,
Is a pure cup of rich Canary wine,
Which is the Mermaid's now, but shall be mine:
Of which had Horace or Anacreon tasted,
Their lives, as do their lines, 'till now had lasted.
　　　　BEN JONSON: *Inviting a Friend to Supper*

Wine, the cheerer of the heart
And lively refresher of the countenance.
　　　　THOMAS MIDDLETON AND WILLIAM ROWLEY: *The Changeling*
　　　　English dramatist (c. 1570-1627) and English actor
　　　　and playwright (c. 1585-c. 1642)

O for a bowl of fat Canary,
　　Rich Aristippus, sparkling sherry!
Some nectar else from Juno's dairy;
　　O these draughts would make us merry!
　　　　THOMAS MIDDLETON

The best wine comes out of an old vessel.
　　　　ROBERT BURTON: *The Anatomy of Melancholy*
　　　　English scholar, clergyman, and writer (1577-1640)

Wine is one thing, drunkenness another.
　　　　ROBERT BURTON

Wine works the heart up, wakes the wit;
There is no cure 'gainst age but it:
It helps the head-ache, cough, and tisic,
And is for all diseases physic.

> JOHN FLETCHER AND FRANCIS BEAUMONT: *The Bloody Brother*
> English dramatists (1579-1625) and (1584-1616)

'Tis late and cold, stir up the fire,
Sit close and draw the table nigher;
Be merry, and drink wine that's old,
A hearty medicine 'gainst the cold.

> JOHN FLETCHER: *The Dead Host's Welcome*

If God forbade drinking would He have made wine so good?

> ARMAND CARDINAL DE RICHELEAU: *Mirame*
> French minister (1585-1642)

O thou the drink of Gods, and Angels! Wine.

> ROBERT HERRICK: *His fare-well to Sack*
> English poet (1591-1674)

If I write a verse, or two,
'Tis with very much ado;
In regard I want that Wine,
Which sho'd conjure up a line.

> ROBERT HERRICK: *To Sir Clipsebie Crewe*

Where Mirth and Friends are absent when we Dine
Or Sup, there wants the Incense and the Wine.

> ROBERT HERRICK: *Meat without Mirth*

Drink Wine, and live here blithefull, while ye may:
The morrowes life too late is, Live to day.

> ROBERT HERRICK: *To Youth*

O Bacchus! let us be
From cares and trouble free;
And thou shalt heare how we
Will chant new Hymnes to thee.

ROBERT HERRICK: *A Hymne to Bacchus*

Fill me my Wine in Christall; thus, and thus
I see't in's puris naturalibus:
Unmixt. I love to have it smirke and shine,
'Tis sin I know, 'tis sin to throtle Wine.

The sun shall no more dispense,
What Mad-man's he, that when it sparkles so,
Will coole his flames, or quench his fires with snow?

ROBERT HERRICK: *How he would drinke his Wine*

ANACREONTICK VERSE

Brisk methinks I am, and fine,
When I drinke my capring wine:
Then to love I do encline;
When I drinke my wanton wine:
And I wish all maidens mine,
When I drinke my sprightly wine:
Well I sup, and well I dine,
When I drinke my frolick wine:
But I languish, lowre, and Pine,
When I want my fragrant wine.

ROBERT HERRICK

You cannot know wine by the barrel.

GEORGE HERBERT: *Jacula Prudentum*
English poet and clergyman (1593-1633)

Wine ever pays for his lodging.

GEORGE HERBERT: *Jacula Prudentum*

Old wine and an old friend are good provisions.
GEORGE HERBERT: *Jacula Prudentum*

Who knows not Love, let him assay
And taste that juice, which on the crosse a pike
Did set again abroach; then let him say
    If ever he did taste the like.
Love is that liquor sweet and most divine,
Which my God feels as bloud; but I, as wine.
GEORGE HERBERT: *The Agonie*

But can he want the grape, who hath the wine?
    I have their fruit and more.
Blessed be God, who prosper'd Noah's vine,
        And made it bring forth grapes good store,
        But much more him I must adore,
Who of the Law's sowre juice sweet wine did make,
Ev'n God himself being pressed for my sake.
GEORGE HERBERT: *The Bunch of Grapes*

The wine in the bottle does not quench thirst.
GEORGE HERBERT

Good wine makes good blood, good blood causeth good
humours, good humours causeth good thoughts, good
thoughts bring forth good works, good works carry a man to
Heaven; ergo good wine carrieth a man to Heaven.
JAMES HOWELL
English author (c. 1594-1666)

A bowl of wine is wondrous good cheer
To make one blithe, buxom, and debonair.
THOMAS RANDOLPH: *The Jealous Lovers*
English poet (1605-35)

We care not for money, riches, or wealth;
Old sack is our money, old sack is our wealth.

THOMAS RANDOLPH

Sacke is the life and soul and spirit of man, the fire which Prometheus stole, not from Jove's kitchen, but his wine-cellar, to increase the native heat and radicall moisture, without which we are but drousie dust and dead clay. This is nectar, the very nepenthe the gods were drunk with: 'tis this that gave Gannymede beauty, Hebe youth, to Jove his heavens and eternity. Do you think Aristotle ever drank perry? or Plato cyder? Do you think Alexander had ever conquered the world if he had been sober? He knew the force and valour of sacke; that it was the best armour, the best encouragement, and that none could be a commander that was not double drunk with wine and ambition.

THOMAS RANDOLPH: *The Jovial Philosopher*

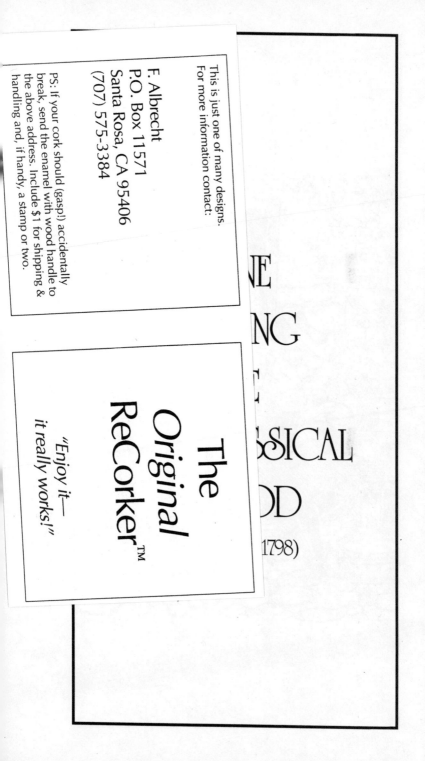

This is just one of many designs.
For more information contact:

F. Albrecht
P.O. Box 11571
Santa Rosa, CA 95406
(707) 575-3384

PS: If your cork should (gasp!) accidentally break, send the enamel with wood handle to the above address. Include $1 for shipping & handling and, if handy, a stamp or two.

The
Original
ReCorker™

*"Enjoy it—
it really works!"*

NE
NG
SICAL
OD
(1798)

THE EIGHTEENTH CENTURY was an important and vital period for the wine industry, particularly in France. It was during this time that first-growth crus and the chateaux of the Bordeaux came into being, thus establishing this region as the premiere wine-producing area of the world. Varietal wines became important, and the Bordeaux wines flourished as the region expanded and more vineyards were planted. The wines of the Burgundy region also developed during this period and emerged as very fine quality wines in their own right.

Champagne had become the drink of monarchs during the reign of Louis XIV in the previous century, and Louis XV faithfully carried on the tradition. The wine trade of France prospered as new markets were developed in Russia, Scandinavia, North America, Africa, and India.

As exploration of the world continued, the grapevine spread to other continents. The eighteenth century witnessed the arrival of *vitis vinifera* in Australia and California, both of which were to become great wine-producing regions.

The Spanish conquistadores had brought vines to Mexico in the early sixteenth century in order to make wine for the celebration of their Catholic masses. As the Franciscan monasteries travelled northward, so did the vine. In 1769, the Franciscan friar Father Junipero Serra established a mission near what is now San Diego, and planted the first Californian vineyards. The vines were a type of *vitis vinifera* which came to be known as the Mission grape. Although it did not make particularly good wines, it was a reliable producer and fulfilled the needs of the friars. Other missions were eventually established, and soon viticulture was firmly rooted along North America's west coast.

Wine, one sip of this will bathe the drooping spirits in
delight beyond the bliss of dreams. Be wise and taste.

> JOHN MILTON
> English poet (1608-74)

Lords are lordliest in their wine.

> JOHN MILTON: *Samson Agonistes*

For he that loveth wine, wanteth no woes.

> ANNE BRADSTREET: *Of the Four Ages of Man*
> Puritan poet and first American woman writer (1612-72)

I'll carve your name on barks of trees
With true-Love-Knots, and flourishes,
That shall infuse eternal spring
And everlasting flourishing
Drink every letter o' it in stum,
And make it brisk Champaign become.

> SAMUEL BUTLER: *Hudibras*
> English writer and satirist (1612-80)

O let me suck the wine
So long of this chast vine
Till drunk of the dear wounds, I be
A lost Thing to the world, as it to me.

> RICHARD CRASHAW: *Sancta Maria Dolorum*
> English religious poet (c. 1613-49)

When Christ, at Cana's feast, by power divine,
Inspired cold water with the warmth of wine,
"See," cried they, while in reddening tide it gushed,
The conscious water saw its God and blushed.

> RICHARD CRASHAW: *Epigrammationa Sacra*

Within this bottle's to be seen
A scarlet liquor that has been
   Born of the royal Vine;
We but nickname it when we call
It God's drink, who drink none at all,
No higher name than Wine.

      ALEXANDER BROME: *On Claret*
      English poet (1620-66)

Of all the rare juices.
That Bacchus or Caeres produces,
There's none that I can, nor dare I
Compare with the princely Canary
For this is the thing
That a fancy infuses,
This first got a King,
And next the nine Muses,
'Twas this made old Poets so sprightly to sing.
And fill all the world with the glory and fame on't.
They Helicon call'd it and the Thespian spring,
But this was the drink, though they knew not the name on't.

      ALEXANDER BROME: *On Canary*

Drink deep: this cup be pregnant; and the wine
Spirit of wit, to make us all divine,
That big with sack and mirth we may retyre
Possessors of more soules, and nobler fire;
And by the influxe of this painted skie,
And labour'd formes, to higher matters flye;
So, if a nap shall take us, we shall all,
    After full cups have dreames poeticall.
Let's laugh now and the pres't grape drinke,
    Till the drowsie day-starre winke.
And in our merry, mad mirth run
    Faster and further than the sun;

And let none his cup forsake,
    Till that star again doth wake;
So we men below shall move
Equally with the gods above.

      HENRY VAUGHAN: *A Rhapsodie*
      British mystic poet (1622-95)

In a golden pitcher let me
Head and ears for comfort get me,
And drink of the vine of the wine benign
That sparkles warm in Sansovine.

      FRANCESCO REDI
      Italian physicist, naturalist, and poet (1626-97)

A good, formall, precise Monister in the Isle of Wight us't to say that a glasse or two of wine extraordinaire would make a man praise God with much alacritie.

      SIR NICOLAS L'ESTRANGE
      (1630-55)

Gentlemen, pray be seated. The wine is at your elbows and your carriages within a hiccup's call.

      LA MARQUISE DE BRINVILLIERS
      Notorious French poisoner (1630-76)

There's nothing but Bacchus
Right merry can make us,
    That virtue particular is to the vine;
It fires ev'ry creature
With wit and good-nature;
    Whose thoughts can be dark when their noses do shine?

      CHARLES COTTON
      English poet (1630-87)

The praise of Bacchus then the sweet musician sung,
Of Bacchus—ever fair and ever young:
The jolly god in triumph comes;
Sound the trumpets; beat the drums:
Flushed with a purple grace
He shows his honest face:
Now give the hautboys breath. He comes! he comes!
Bacchus ever fair and ever young,
Drinking joys did first ordain;
Bacchus' blessings are a treasure,
Drinking is the soldier's pleasure.
Rich the treasure,
Sweet the pleasure,
Sweet is pleasure after pain.

JOHN DRYDEN: *Alexander's Feast*
English poet (1631-1700)

The pleasures of love and the joys of good wine,
To perfect our happiness wisely we join.
We to beauty all day
Give the sovereign sway
And her Favorite nymphs devoutly obey.
At the plays we are constantly making our court,
And when they are ended we follow the sport
To the Mall and the Park
Where we love till 'tis dark,
Then sparkling Champaign
Puts an end to their reign;
It quickly recovers
Poor languishing lovers,
Makes us frolic and gay, and drowns all sorrow;
But alas we relapse again on the morrow.
Let every man stand
With his glass in his hand,
And briskly discharge at the word of command.
Here's a health to all those
Whom tonight we depose:
Wine and beauty by turns great souls should inspire.
Present all together—and now, boys, give fire!

SIR GEORGE ETHEREGE: *Song*
English dramatist (c. 1635-92)

I within did flow
With seas of life like wine.
> THOMAS TRAHERNE: *Wonder*
> English poet (c. 1636-74)

Come quickly, I am tasting stars!
> DOM PERIGNON: *upon first tasting champagne*
> French Benedictine monk (1638-1715)

Since you no longer will be kind,
  But my embraces shun,
Bacchus shall ease my am'rous mind,
  To his embrace I run.

Wine gives a pleasure unrestrain'd,
  Dispells the frantic spleen;
Tho' wishes cannot be attain'd,
Looks are still joyful seen.
> SIR CHARLES SEDLEY: *To Phyllis, Who Slighted Him*
> English wit, poet, and dramatist (c. 1639-1701)

Drink in itself is a good creature of God and to be received
with thankfulness, but the abuse of drink is from Satan; the
wine is from God but the drunkard is from the Devil.
> INCREASE MATHER
> American minister (1639-1723)

Come, lay by your cares, and hang up your sorrow;
Drink on, he's a sot that e'er thinks on tomorrow;
Good store of good claret supplies everything,
And the man that is drunk is as great as a king.

Let none at misfortune or losses repine,
But take a full dose of the juice of the vine;
Diseases and troubles are ne'er to be found,
But in the damned place where the glass goes not round.
> THOMAS SHADWELL: *The Miser*
> English playwright and poet (1640-92)

Wine gives you liberty, love takes it away.

WILLIAM WYCHERLY: *The Country Wife*
English dramatist (c. 1640-1716)

Cupid and Bacchus my saints are;
    May drink and love still reign!
With wine I wash away my care
    And then to love again.

JOHN WILMOT, EARL OF ROCHESTER: *Upon Drinking in a Bowl*
English courtier and poet (1647-80)

If all be true that I do think,
There are five reasons we should drink:
Good wine—a friend—or being dry—
Or lest we should be by and by—
Or any other reason why.

HENRY ALDRICH: *Five Reasons for Drinking*
English scholar and dean of Christ Church (1647-1710)

A friend and a bottle is all my design;
He has no room for treason that's top-full of wine.

JOHN OLDHAM: *The Careless Goodfellow*
English poet (1653-83)

Drink on, drink on, drink on till night be spent and sun do shine,
Did not the gods give anxious mortals wine
To wash all care and troubles from the heart,
Why then so soon should jovial fellows part?
Come, let this bumper for the next make way;
Who's sure to live and drink another day?

HENRY PURCELL
English composer (1659-95)

He that drinks is immortal
For wine still supplies
What age wears away;
How can he be dust
That moistens his clay?
>
> HENRY PURCELL

With nobler products see thy Georgia teems
Cheered with the genial sun's director beams;
There the wild vine to culture learns to yield,
And purple clusters ripen through the field.
Now bid thy merchants bring thy wine no more
Or from the Iberian or the Tuscan shore;
No more thy needs the Hungarian vineyards drain,
And France herself may drink her best Champagne.
Behold! at last, and in a subject land,
Nectars sufficient for thy large demand.
>
> SAMUEL WESLEY
> American poet and divine (1662-1735)

Wine whets the Wit, improves its Native force,
And gives a pleasant flavor to Discourse.
By making all our spirits Debonair,
Throws off the Lees, the sediment of Care.
>
> JOHN POMFRET: *The Choice*
> English poet (1667-1702)

This wine should be eaten, it is too good to be drunk.
>
> JONATHAN SWIFT: *Polite Conversation*
> English satirist (1667-1745)

The first glass[of wine] for myself, the second for my friends,
the third for good humor, and the fourth for mine enemies.
>
> JOSEPH ADDISON: *The Spectator No. 195*
> English essayist and playwright (1672-1719)

Malice ne'er spoke in generous Champaign.
The privilege of wine we only ask,
You'll taste again before you damn the flask.

GEORGE FARQUHAR: *The Constant Couple*
Irish playwright (1677-1707)

Wine makes love forget its care,
And mirth exalts a feast.

THOMAS PARNELL
Anglo-Irish poet (1679-1718)

To the expecting mouth, with grateful taste,
The ebbing wine glides swiftly o'er the tongue.

JOHN GAY
English poet and dramatist (1685-1732)

Name, Sirs, the WINE that most invites your Tast,
Champaign or Burgundy, or Florence pure,
Or Hock Antique, or Lisbon New or Old,
Bordeaux, or neat French White, or Alicant:
For Bordeaux we with Voice Unanimous
Declare, (such Sympathy's in Boon Compeers.)
He quits the Room Alert, but soon returns,
One Hand Capacious glist'ring Vessels bore
Resplendant, th' other with a grasp secure,
A Bottle (mighty charge) upstaid, full Fraught
With goodly Wine, He with extended Hand
Rais'd high, pours forth the Sanguin frothy Juice,
O'respread with Bubbles, dissipated soon:
We strait t' our Arms repair, experienc't Chiefs;
Now Glasses clash with Glasses, (charming sound,)
And Glorious ANNA's Health the first the best
Crowns the full Glass, at HER inspiring Name
The sprightly Wine Results, and seems to Smile,
With hearty Zeal, and wish Unanimous
The Health we Drink, and in HER Health our own.

JOHN GAY: *Wine, A Poem*

Wine can clear
The vapors of despair,
And make us light as air.

> JOHN GAY: *The Beggar's Opera*

Fill ev'ry glass, for wine inspires us,
And fires us
With courage, love, and joy.
Women and wine should life employ.
Is there aught else on earth desirous?

> JOHN GAY: *The Beggar's Opera*

Man can die
Much bolder with brandy.

> JOHN GAY: *The Beggar's Opera*

From wine what sudden friendship springs!

> JOHN GAY: *The Squire and His Cur*

A BACCHANAL

Bacchus, god of mortal pleasure,
Ever give me of thy treasure.
How I long for t'other quart,
Ring and call the drowsy waiter
Hither since it is no later,
Why should good companions part?

Whip a shilling he that's willing,
Follow this example round.
If you'd wear a lib'ral spirit,
Put about the generous claret,
After death no smiling's found.

> GEORGE FRIDERIC HANDEL
> German composer (1685-1759)

A Bacchanalian Rant

Bacchus must his power resign—
I am the only God of Wine!
It is not fit the wretch should be
In competition set with me,
Who can drink ten times more than he.

Make a new world, ye powers divine!
Stocked with nothing else but wine:
Let wine its only product be,
Let wine be earth, and air, and sea—
And let that wine be all for me.

Let other mortals vainly wear
A tedious life in anxious care;
Let the ambitious toil and think;
Let states or empires swim or sink;
My sole ambition is to drink.

> HENRY CAREY
> English poet and composer (1687-1743)

Wine awakens and refreshes the lurking passions of the mind.

> ALEXANDER POPE: *Persuasive*
> English poet (1688-1744)

Wine lets no lover unrewarded go.

> ALEXANDER POPE: *The Wife of Bath*

Give me Champagne and fill it to the brim,
I'll toast in bumpers ev'ry lovely limb;
I challenge all the heroes of the skies
To show a goddess with a Craven's eyes.
Why then averse to love? Ah, leave disdain,
Discard thy fickle undeserving swain,
And pledge thy lover in the brisk Champaign.

> LORD CHESTERFIELD: *Witticisms*
> English statesman and writer (1694-1773)

Chloris and Egles are pouring for me
With their own hand
A good wine of Ay, whose captive bubble
Sprang forth from the bottle
And with lightning speed has thrust the cork away.

> FRANCOIS VOLTAIRE
> French satirist, author, and historian (1694-1778)

The sparkling froth of the wine of Ay
And the yellow liquer of Tokay
In arousing the fibers of the brain
Bring to the mind a fire that is expressed in beautiful words
As brilliant as the light liquid that rises and leaps and foams
up the edge of the glass.

> FRANCOIS VOLTAIRE

Wine is the divine juice of September.

> FRANCOIS VOLTAIRE

I serve your Beaune to all my friends, but your Volnay I keep
for myself.

> FRANCOIS VOLTAIRE: *letter to Louis Latour*

In smiling Bacchus' joys I'll roll,
Deny no pleasures to my soul;
Let Bacchus' health round briskly move,
But Bacchus is a friend to love.
And he that will this health deny,
Down among the dead men let him lie!
Let love and wine their rights maintain,
And their united pleasures reign,
While Bacchus' treasures crown the board,
We'll sing the joys that both afford;
And they who won't with us comply—
Down among the dead men let them lie,

> JOHN DYER
> British poet (1700-58)

Wine is the noblest cordial of nature.
JOHN WESLEY
English dramatist (1703-91)

Wine makes daily living easier, less hurried, with fewer tensions and more tolerance.
BENJAMIN FRANKLIN
American author, scientist, and statesman (1706-90)

We hear of the conversions of water into wine at the marriage in Cana as a miracle. But this conversion is, through the goodness of God, made every day before our eyes. Behold the rain which descends from heaven upon the vineyards, and which enters into the vine roots to be changed into wine, a constant proof that God loves us and loves to see us happy.
BENJAMIN FRANKLIN: *Letter to Abbe Morlay*

Take counsel in wine, but resolve afterwards in water.
BENJAMIN FRANKLIN: *Poor Richard's Almanac*

'Twas Noah who first planted the vine
And mended his Morals by drinking its wine.
BENJAMIN FRANKLIN: *A Drinking Song*

Wine gives great pleasure, and every pleasure is of itself good.
SAMUEL JOHNSON: *Boswell's Life*
English lexicographer, critic, and poet (1709-84)

Claret is the liquor for boys; port for men; but he who aspires to be a hero must drink brandy.
SAMUEL JOHNSON: *Boswell's Life*

He who aspires to be a serious wine drinker
must drink claret.

SAMUEL JOHNSON

I think wealth has lost much of its value if it have not the
whimsical sallies of wit that are the natural productions of
Champagne.

SARAH FIELDING: *The Countess of Dellwyn*
English writer (1710-68)

The rarest virtue that a single lady can possess—the virtue of
putting wine on the table.

WILLIAM COLLINS: *I Say No*
English lyric poet (1721-59)

Champagne is the only wine a woman can drink and still
remain beautiful.

MADAME POMPADOUR
Mistress of Louis XV (1721-64)

The wine cannot be bad where the company is agreeable.

TOBIAS SMOLLET: *Humphrey Clinker*
Scottish novelist (1721-71)

The doctor he gave me some Spanish quinine:
All his powders were wasted, my body was lean,
The Hungarian cure made me feel hale and fine,
I was cured by my cellar's fifteen-year-old wine!

JOZSEF GVADANYI
Hungarian poet (1725-1801)

I love everything that's old: old friends, old times, old man-
ners, old books, old wines.

OLIVER GOLDSMITH: *She Stoops to Conquer*
Irish playwright, novelist, and poet (1728-74)

[Wine is] the philosopher which drives away care, and makes us forget whatever is disagreeable.

OLIVER GOLDSMITH

For without love or wine, now own!
What wouldst thou be, O man! A stone.

GOTTHOLD LESSING
German dramatist and critic (1729-81)

My manner of living is plain, a glass of wine and a bit of mutton are always ready, and such as will be content to partake of that are always welcome.

GEORGE WASHINGTON
American president, general, and oenophile (1732-99)

We'll drink then on the Cape of Hope
Its golden juice divine,
And then with yearning hearts and true
We'll think, O distant friends, of you
And mix our tears with wine.

CHRISTIAN SCHUBART
German musician and poet (1739-91)

In certain studies there is no harm in doing one's thinking and writing while slightly drunk, and then revising one's work in cold blood. The stimulus of wine is favourable to the play of invention, and to fluency of expression.

G. C. LICHTENBERG: *Reflections*
German physicist and satirist (1742-99)

I have lived temperately, eating little animal food. Vegetables constitute my principal diet. I double, however, the doctor's glass and a half of wine, and even treble it with a friend!

THOMAS JEFFERSON: *Letter to President Monroe*
American president, philosopher, and vintner (1743-1826)

Good wine is a necessity of life for me.

THOMAS JEFFERSON: *Letter to John Adlum*

Fix but the duty... and we can drink wine here as cheap as we do grog; and who will not prefer it? Its extended use will carry health and comfort to a much enlarged circle.

THOMAS JEFFERSON: *Letter to M. de Neuville*

No nation is drunken where wine is cheap; and none sober where the dearness of wine substitutes ardent spirits as the common beverage. It is in truth the only antidote to the bane of whiskey.

THOMAS JEFFERSON: *Letter to M. de Neuville*

I think it is a great error to consider a heavy tax on wines as a tax on luxury. On the contrary, it is a tax on the health of our citizens.

THOMAS JEFFERSON

We could, in the United States, make as great a variety of wines as are made in Europe, not exactly the same kinds, but doubtless as good.

THOMAS JEFFERSON

Grapes the vine-stock bears!
Horns the buck-goat wears,
Wine is sap, the vine is wood,
The table yieldeth wine as good.
With a deeper glance and true
The mysteries of nature view!
Have faith, and here's a miracle!
Your stoppers draw and drink your fill.

JOHANN WOLFGANG VON GOETHE
German poet, writer, and scientist (1749-1832)

Wine rejoices in the heart of man, and joy is the mother of every virtue. When thou hast drunk wine, thou art ever double what thou wouldst otherwise be—twice as full of ingenuity, twice as enterprising, twice as energetic.

JOHANN WOLFGANG VON GOETHE: Goetz von Berlichingen

I carry on mental dialogues with the shoots of the grapevine, who reveal to me grand thoughts, and to whom I can retell wondrous things.

JOHANN WOLFGANG VON GOETHE: Faust

What man can pretend to be a believer in love, who is an abjurer of wine?

RICHARD B. SHERIDAN: The School for Scandal
Irish playwright and politician (1751-1816)

Truth, they say, lies in a well,
Why, I vow I ne'er could see;
Let the water-drinkers tell,
There it always lay for me.
For when sparkling wine went round,
Never saw I falsehood's mask;
But still honest truth I found
In the bottom of each flask.

RICHARD B. SHERIDAN: The Duenna

This bottle's the sun of our table,
His beams are rosy wine;
We planets that are not able
Without his help to shine.

RICHARD B. SHERIDAN: The Duenna

A man may surely be allowed to take a glass of wine by his own fireside.

RICHARD B. SHERIDAN: drinking a glass of wine in the street while watching his Drury Lane theatre burn down

A Bacchanalian

What is war and all its joys?
Useless mischief, empty noise.

What are arms and trophies won?
Spangles glittering in the sun.
Rosy Bacchus, give me wine,
Happiness is only thine!

What is love without the bowl?
'Tis a languor of the soul.
Crowned with ivy, Venus charms;
Ivy courts me to her arms.
Bacchus, give me love and wine,
Happiness is only thine!

        THOMAS CHATTERTON
        English poet (1752-1770)

Count all the trees that crown Jamaica's hills,
Count all the stars that through the heavens you see,
Count every drop that the wide ocean fills;
Then count the pleasures Bacchus yields to me.

        PHILIP FRENEAU: *The Jamaica Funeral*
        American sailor and poet (1752-1832)

Wine, like the rising sun, possession gains,
And drives the mist of dullness from the brains;
The gloomy vapor from the spirit flies,
And views of gaiety and gladness rise.

        GEORGE CRABBE: *The Borough*
        English poet (1754-1832)

Wine, the most agreeable of beverages, whether we owe it
to Noah who planted the first vine, or Bacchus who pressed
the first grapes, dates from the beginning of the world.

        ANTHELME BRILLAT-SAVARIN: *The Physiology of Taste*
        French lawyer, writer, and gastronome (1755-1826)

A meal without wine is like a day without sunshine.
ANTHELME BRILLAT-SAVARIN: *The Physiology of Taste*

The discovery of wine is of greater moment than the discovery of a constellation. The universe is too full of stars.
ANTHELME BRILLAT-SAVARIN: *The Physiology of Taste*

After a fine meal, a wine connoisseur was offered some grapes for dessert. "Thank you," said he, pushing the dish away from him, "But I am not in the habit of taking my wine in pills."
ANTHELME BRILLAT-SAVARIN: *The Physiology of Taste*

Wine is the milk of the old, the balm of adults and the vehicle of the gourmand.
A. B. L. GRIMOND DE LA REYNIERE
(1758-1837)

Let's drink to the days that we love to recall,
     And pledge in this good wine;
Let's drink to the days that were best of all,
     The days of Auld Lang Syne.
ROBERT BURNS: *Auld Lang Syne*
Scottish poet (1759-96)

Fill me with the rosy wine,
Call a toast, a toast divine.
ROBERT BURNS: *The Toast*

In introducing this grape to public notice, I have done my country a greater service than I should have done, had I paid the national debt.
JOHN ADLUM
American viticulturalist (1759-1836)

Clearly, the pleasures wines afford are transitory—but so are those of the ballet, or of a musical performance. Wine is inspiring and adds greatly to the joy of living.

NAPOLEON I
French general and emperor (1769-1821)

Nothing makes the future look so rosy as to contemplate it through a glass of Chambertin.

NAPOLEON I

In victory you deserve [champagne], in defeat you need it.

NAPOLEON I

A glass of wine is a great refreshment after a hard day's work.

LUDWIG VON BEETHOVEN
German composer (1770-1827)

The enjoyment of wine comes from the thunderous god.

FRIEDRICH HOLDERLIN: *Brod und Wein*
German poet (1770-1843)

The juice of the grape is given to him that will use it wisely, as that which cheers the heart of man after toil, refreshes him in sickness and comforts him in sorrow. He who so enjoyeth it may thank God for his wine-cup as for his daily bread; and he who abuseth the gift of heaven is not a greater fool in his intoxication than thou in thine abstinence.

SIR WALTER SCOTT
Scottish novelist, poet, and historian (1771-1832)

A glass of good wine is a gracious creature, and reconciles poor mortality to itself, and that is what few things can do.

SIR WALTER SCOTT: *Journal*

Wine, I am sure, good, mellow, generous port, can hurt nobody—unless those who take it to excess, which they may easily avoid, if they observe the rules of temperance.

CHARLES LAMB
English essayist and author (1775-1834)

May our lives, tho' alas!—like the wine of tonight,
They must soon have an end,—to the last, flow as bright!

THOMAS MOORE
Irish poet (1779-1852)

Say, why did Time
His glass sublime
Fill up with sands unsightly?
When wine he knew
Runs brisker through,
And sparkles far more brightly.
Oh, lend it us,
And smiling thus,
The glass in two we'd sever,
Make pleasure glide
In double tide,
And fill both ends forever.
Then wreathe the bowl
With flowers of soul
The brightest wit can find us,
We'll take a flight
Towards heav'n tonight
And leave dull earth behind us.

THOMAS MOORE

If with water you fill up your glasses,
You'll never write anything wise;
For wine is the horse of Parnassus,
Which hurries a bard to the skies.

THOMAS MOORE: *Anacreontic*

113

Oh, if delight could charm no more,
If all the goblet's bliss were o'er,
When fate had once our doom decreed,
Then dying would be death indeed!
Nor could I think, unblest by wine,
Divinity itself divine.

THOMAS MOORE

Press the grape, and let it pour
Around the board its purple shower;
And while the drops my goblet steep,
I'll think—in woe the clusters weep.

Weep on, weep on, my pouting vine!
Heaven grant no tears, but tears of wine.
Weep on; and as thy sorrows flow,
I'll taste the luxury of woe!

THOMAS MOORE: *Juvenile Poems*

What though youth gave love and roses,
Age still leaves us friends and wine.

THOMAS MOORE: *Spring and Autumn*

For in the hand of the Lord there is a cup, and the wine is red;
it is full mixt, and he poureth out of the same.

THE BOOK OF COMMON PRAYER 75:9
(c. 1789)

WINE DURING THE ROMANTIC ERA

(c. 1798 - c. 1870)

THE ROMANTIC PERIOD proved to be the best of times and the worst of times for wine. Technological advances were many, wine-making became an important enterprise in South America and the United States, and fine vintage ports were produced in Portugal. The European wine industry boomed, particularly in France, and some of the finest French wines ever made were from the period between 1830 and 1880.

The technological advances achieved during the nineteenth century were significant to the development of the wine industry. Bottles were used more and more, not only for storing wine, but also for selling it to the consumer. Previously, bottles had to be made by hand. They were costly and somewhat fragile, and, therefore, only used by the more prestigious chateaux. With the advent of molded bottles the sale of wine was revolutionized. The bottles offered a neutral container which enhanced the aging process. They also allowed the consumer to buy wines in reasonable amounts (rather than by the cask), which could be stored without worry of deterioration. Furthermore, by using colored glass, harmful light rays could be filtered out, thereby helping to preserve the wine.

The growth of the bottle industry, in combination with advancements in the use of corks as stoppers, ensured a golden era for wine. Not since the Romans had the possibility of true vintage wines been a reality. Technological skills which had long ago been discovered and mastered by those ancient winemakers had been forgotten, but were reborn during this period.

Other major advancements in the technology of winemaking included scientist Louis Pasteur's discovery of the nature of fermentation in the mid-1800s. Until then, this process had been a mystery—no one really knew what caused the juice from crushed grapes to turn into wine. Pasteur discovered the presence of microscopic yeasts on the skins of grapes which, when combined with the sugar of the juice, produced alcohol and carbon dioxide.

With this simple realization, the winemaker could have more control over the fermentation process, and thus, over the finished product. The art of winemaking was transformed into a science, thereby rendering nature a less formidable opponent in the process of creating fine wines. However, nature was not so easily mastered for this was the era of the dreaded phylloxera, the vine louse.

Transported to Europe via the imported native American species of vine, which was immune to it, the phylloxera quickly spread through the *vitis vinifera* vineyards there. By the end of the 1870s, the vineyards of the great Bordeaux region had been completely destroyed. Those of the Champagne and Burgundy districts were devastated within the following decade. The damage was enormous and costly. Millions of acres of vineyards had to be torn up and replanted with *vitis vinifera* vines which had been grafted onto the native American rootstock of *vitis labrusca*. It took France over fifty years to recover. California was more fortunate.

In the 1830s, Jean-Louis Vignes brought European vines to the west coast of North America, and the wine industry began to develop there. The eastern United States produced wines of fairly good quality from *vitis labrusca* grapes which had been hybridized by early European imports, and the Great Lakes area was a busy winemaking region. In fact, in 1859 Ohio produced twice as much wine as California. That was soon to change, however.

In the 1860s, Hungarian immigrant Agoston Haraszthy imported over 100,000 European vines of 300 varieties, and California viticulture was born. The influx of European immigrants, with their rich, cultural heritage of wine, contributed immensely to the development of the wine industry. Many of the wineries established during this period still exist today and have a long history of producing wines of exceptional quality. Inglenook, established in 1887 by Gustave Niebaum, Beringer in 1895 by Frederich and Jacob Beringer, and Beaulieu in 1899 by Georges de Latour are all prime examples.

During the nineteenth century, the California vineyards were also affected by the phylloxera, but not to the extent Europe's were. The louse was discovered in the late 1800s, and because it spread slowly there, the Californians were able to combat it by gradually replacing their existing vines with the grafted rootstocks. The battle was costly and time-consuming, but was not devastating to the newly-developing wine industry.

Unfortunately, just as California was recovering from its attack of phylloxera, a new enemy appeared. A mysterious virus-like disease, called the Anaheim disease after its place of origin, invaded the vineyards, and in the decade between 1884 and 1894 over 30,000 acres were destroyed. The California winemakers persevered and replanted their vineyards once again, not knowing that their most dangerous enemy of all time loomed on the horizon of the twentieth century.

If your heart fail you, another cup of wine will set all to rights.
THOMAS LOVE PEACOCK: *The Misfortunes of Elfin*
English novelist and poet (1785-1866)

There are two reasons for drinking [wine]. . . when you are thirsty, to cure it; the other, when you are not thirsty, to prevent it. . . prevention is better than cure.
THOMAS LOVE PEACOCK: *Melincour*

A bottle of Champagne
Frozen into a very vinous ice,
   Which leaves few drops of that immortal rain;
Yet in the very center, past all price,
   About a liquid glassful will remain;
And this is stronger than the strongest grape
Could e'er express in its expanded shape:

'Tis the whole spirit brought to a quintessence;
   And thus the chilliest aspects may concentre
A hidden nectar under a cold presence.
LORD BYRON: *Don Juan*
English poet (1788-1824)

Sweet is the vintage, when the showering grapes
In Bacchanal profusion reel to earth,
Purple and gushing.
LORD BYRON: *Don Juan*

The evaporation of a joyous day
   Is like the last glass of Champaigne, without
The foam which made its virgin bumper gay.
LORD BYRON: *Don Juan*

Sweet is old wine in bottles.
LORD BYRON: *Don Juan*

120

Champaign with foaming whirls
As white as Cleopatra's melted pearls.
LORD BYRON: *Don Juan*

Long life to the grape! for when summer is flown,
The age of our nectar shall gladden our own;
We must die. Who shall not?
May our sins be forgiven,
And Hebe shall never be idle in heaven!
LORD BYRON: *Fill the Goblet Again*

Man, being reasonable, must get drunk;
The best of life is but intoxication,—
Glory, the grape, love, gold,—in these are sunk
The hopes of all men, and of every nation.
LORD BYRON

Wine, which cheers the sad, revives the old, inspires
The young, makes Weariness forget his toil,
And fear, her danger, opens a new world
When this, the present palls!
LORD BYRON

Where once my wit, perchance, hath shone,
In aid of others let me shine;
And when, alas! our brains are gone
What nobler substitute than wine.
LORD BYRON

The very best of vineyards is the cellar.
LORD BYRON

Few things surpass old wine; and they may preach
Who please, the more because they preach in vain.
LORD BYRON

Here's a bumper of wine; fill thine, fill mine:—
Here's a health to old Noah, who planted the vine!

RICHARD HARRIS BARHAM
English humorist (1788-1845)

Sing!—who sings
To her who weareth a hundred rings?
Ah, who is this fine lady?
The Vine, boys, the Vine!
The mother of mighty wine.
A roamer is she
O'er wall and tree,
And sometimes very good company.

Drink!—who drinks
To her who blusheth and never thinks?
Ah! who is this maid of thine?
The Grape, boys, the Grape!
Until she be turned to Wine!
For better is she
Than Vine can be,
And very, very good company.

Dream!—who dreams
Of the God that governs a thousand streams?
Ah! who is this spirit fine?
'Tis Wine, boys, 'tis Wine!
God Bacchus, a friend of mine.
O, better is he
Than Grape or tree,
And the best of all good company.

BARRY CORNWALL
English poet (1789-1874)

My brain is swimming round;
Give me a bowl of wine!

PERCY BYSSHE SHELLEY: *The Cenci*
English poet (1792-1822)

O, thou bright wine whose purple splendor leaps
And bubbles gaily in this golden bowl
Under the lamplight as my spirits do.
PERCY BYSSHE SHELLEY: *The Cenci*

Fill up this goblet with Greek wine. I said
I would not drink this evening; but I must;
For, strange to say, I find my spirits fail
With thinking what I have decreed to do.
PERCY BYSSHE SHELLEY: *The Cenci*

I filled
The cup of Maron, and I offered him
To taste, and said:—'Child of the Ocean God,
Behold what drink the vines of Greece produce,
The exultation and the joy of Bacchus.'
PERCY BYSSHE SHELLEY: *The Cyclops*

Silenus: But how much gold will you engage to give?
Ulysses: I bring no gold, but Bacchic juice.
Silenus: Oh, joy! 'Tis long since these dry lips were wet with
wine.
PERCY BYSSHE SHELLEY: *The Cyclops*

Ha! ha! ha! I'm full of wine,
Heavy with the joy divine.
PERCY BYSSHE SHELLEY: *The Cyclops*

Souls of Poets dead and gone,
What Elysium have ye known,
Happy field or mossy cavern,
Choicer than the Mermaid Tavern?
Have ye tippled drink more fine
Than mine host's Canary wine?
JOHN KEATS: *Lines on the Mermaid Tavern*
English poet (1795-1821)

I like claret. . . . For really 'tis so fine—it fills one's mouth with a gushing freshness—then goes down cool and feverless—then you do not feel it quarrelling with your liver—no, it is rather a Peacemaker, and lies as quiet as it did in the grape; then it is as fragrant as the Queen Bee, and the more ethereal part of it mounts into the Brain, not assaulting the cerebral apartments like a bully in a badhouse looking for his trull, and hurrying from door to door bouncing against the wainscot, but rather walks like Aladdin about his enchanted palace so gently that you do not feel his step.

JOHN KEATS: *Letter to George and Georgina Keats*

O, for a draught of vintage! that hath been
    Cool'd a long age in the deep-delved earth,
Tasting of Flora and the country green,
    Dance, and Provencal song, and sunburnt mirth!
O for a beaker full of the warm South,
    Full of the true, the blushful Hippocrene,
      With beaded bubbles winking at the brim,
        And purple-stained mouth;
    That I might drink, and leave the world unseen,
    And with thee fade away into the forest dim.

JOHN KEATS: *Ode to a Nightingale*

The splendour of the revelries,
When butts of wine are drunk off to the lees.

JOHN KEATS

Men who have communion in nothing else can sympathetically eat together, can still rise into some glow of brotherhood over food and wine.

THOMAS CARLYLE
Scottish essayist and historian (1795-1881)

Drink wine in winter for cold, and in summer for heat.

H. G. BOHN: *Handbook of Proverbs*
British publisher (1796-1884)

He arrives—the cork goes flying up
Wine of the Comet fills the cup.

ALEXANDER PUSHKIN
Russian poet (1799-1837)

The pail is brought, the ice is clinking
Round old Moet or Veuve Clicquot;
This is what poets should be drinking
And they delight to see it flow.
Like Hippocrene it sparkles brightly,
The golden bubbles rising lightly
(The image, why, of this and that:
I quote myself, and do it pat).
I could not see it without gloating,
And once I gave my meagre all
To get it, friends, do you recall?
How many follies then were floating
Upon the magic of that stream—
What verse, what talk, how fair a dream!

But this bright sibilant potation
Betrays my stomach, and although
I love it still, at the dictation
Of prudence now I drink Bordeaux.
Ay is risky, if delicious;
It's like a mistress, gay, capricious,
Enchanting, sparkling, frivolous,
And empty—so it seems to us. . . .
But you, Bordeaux, I always treasure
As a good comrade, one who shares
Our sorrows and our smaller cares,
And also our calm hours of leisure,
One whose warm kindness has no end—
Long live Bordeaux, the faithful friend!

ALEXANDER PUSHKIN: *Eugene Onegin*

It was my father's wine—Alas!
    It was his chiefest bliss
To fill an old friend's evening glass
    With nectar such as this.
I think I have as warm a heart,
    As kind a friend as he;
Another bumper ere we part:
    Old wine, old wine for me!
        WINTHROP MACKWORTH PRAED: *Old Wine*
        English poet (1802-39)

Fill every beaker up, my men, pour forth the cheering
    wine:
There's life and strength in every drop—thanksgiving to
    the vine!
        ALBERT GORTON GREENE: *The Baron's Last Banquet*
        American lawyer and poet (1802-68)

Wine is the intellectual part of a meal, meats are merely the
material part.
        ALEXANDER DUMAS
        French novelist and playwright (1802-70)

Montrachet should be drunk on the knees with the head
bared.
        ALEXANDER DUMAS

At the first sip a good drinker will recognize the vineyard, at
the second the quality, and at the third the year.
        ALEXANDER DUMAS: *La Dame de Monsoreau*

God made only water, but man made wine.
        VICTOR HUGO: *Les Contemplations*
        French poet and author (1802-85)

Bacchus

Bring me wine, but wine which never grew
In the belly of the grape,
Or grew on vine whose tap-roots, reaching through
Under the Andes to the Cape,
Suffer no savor of the earth to scape.

Let its grapes the morn salute
From a nocturnal root,
Which feels the acrid juice
Of Styx and Erebus;
And turns the woe of Night,
By its own craft to a more rich delight.
We buy ashes for bread;
We buy diluted wine;
Give me of the true,—
Whose ample leaves and tendrils curled
Among the silver hills of heaven
Draw everlasting dew;
Wine of wine,
Blood of the world,
Form of forms, and mould of statures,
That I intoxicated,
And by the draught assimilated,
May float at pleasure through all natures;
The bird-language rightly spell,
And that which roses say so well.

Wine that is shed
Like the torrents of the sun
Up the horizon walls,
Or like the Atlantic streams, which run
When the South Sea calls.

Water and bread,
Food which needs no transmuting,
Rainbow-flowering, wisdom-fruiting,
Wine which is already man,
Food which teach and reason can.

Wine which Music is,—
Music and wine are one,—
That I, drinking this,
Shall hear far Chaos talk with me;
Kings unborn shall walk with me;
And the poor grass shall plot and plan
What it will do when it is man.
Quickened so, will I unlock
Every crypt of every rock.

I thank the joyful juice
For all I know;—
Winds of remembering
Of the ancient being blow,
And seeming-solid walls of use
Open and flow.

Pour, Bacchus! the remembering wine;
Retrieve the loss of me and mine!
Vine for vine be antidote,
And the grape requite the lote!
Haste to cure the old despair,—
Reason in Nature's lotus drenched,
The memory of ages quenched;
Give them again to shine;
Let wine repair what this undid;
And where the infection slid,
A dazzling memory revive;
Refresh the faded tints,
Recut the aged prints,
And write my old adventures with the pen
Which on the first day drew,
Upon the tablets blue,
The dancing Pleiads and eternal men.
> RALPH WALDO EMERSON
> American essayist and poet (1803-1882)

A man will be eloquent if you give him good wine.
> RALPH WALDO EMERSON: *Representative Men*

When I heard that Mr. Sturgis had given up wine, I had the same regret that I had in learning Mr. Bowditch had broken his hip.

RALPH WALDO EMERSON

Give me wine to wash me clean
Of the weather-stains of cares.

RALPH WALDO EMERSON: *From the Persian of Hafiz*

A waltz and a glass of wine can invite an encore.

JOHANN STRAUSS
Austrian composer (1804-49)

I rather like bad wine; one gets so bored with good wine.

BENJAMIN DISRAELI: *Sybil*
British statesman and novelist (1804-81)

THE WINE OF JURANCON

Little sweet wine of Jurancon,
    You are dear to my memory still!
With mine host and his merry song,
    Under the rose-tree I drank my fill.

Twenty years after, passing that way,
    Under the trellis I found again
Mine host, still sitting there au frais,
    And singing still the same refrain.

The Jurancon, so fresh and bold,
    Treats me as one it used to know;
Souvenirs of the days of old
    Already from the bottle flow.

With glass in hand our glances met;
    We pledge, we drink. How sour it is!

Never Argenteuil piquette
      Was to my palate as sour as this!

And yet the vintage was good, in sooth;
      The self-same juice, the self-same cask!
It was you, O gayety of my youth,
      That failed in the autumnal flask!
                HENRY WADSWORTH LONGFELLOW
                American poet (1807-82)

CATAWBA WINE

      This song of mine
      Is a Song of the Vine,
To be sung by the glowing embers
      Of wayside inns,
      When the rain begins
To darken the drear Novembers.

      It is not a song
      Of the Scuppernong,
From warm Carolinian valleys,
      Nor the Isabel
      And the Muscadel
That bask in our garden alleys.

      Nor the red Mustang,
      Whose clusters hang
O'er the waves of the Colorado,
      And the fiery flood
      Of whose purple blood
Has a dash of Spanish bravado.

      For richest and best
      Is the wine of the West,
That grows by the Beautiful River;
      Whose sweet perfume
      Fills all the room
With a benison on the giver.

And as hollow trees
Are haunts of bees,
Forever going and coming;
So this crystal hive
Is all alive
With a swarming and buzzing and humming.

Very good in its way
Is the Verzenay,
Or the Sillery soft and creamy;
But a Catawba wine
Has a taste more divine,
More dulcet, delicious, and dreamy.

There grows no vine
By the haunted Rhine,
By Danube or Guadalquivir,
Nor on island or cape,
That bears such a grape
As grows by the Beautiful River.

Drugged is their juice
For foreign use,
When shipped o'er the reeling Atlantic,
To rack our brains
With the fever pains,
That have driven the Old World frantic.

To the sewers and sinks
With all such drinks,
And after them tumble the mixer;
For a poison malign
Is such Borgia wine,
Or at best but a Devil's Elixir.

While pure as a spring
Is the wine I sing,
And to praise it, one needs but name it;
For Catawba wine
Has need of no sign,
Nor tavern-bush to proclaim it.

And this Song of the Vine,
This greeting of mine,
The wind and the birds shall deliver
To the Queen of the West,
In her garlands dressed,
On the banks of the Beautiful River.

HENRY WADSWORTH LONGFELLOW

When you ask one friend to dine,
Give him your best wine!
When you ask two,
The second best will do!

HENRY WADSWORTH LONGFELLOW: *quoted in Brander*
Matthews' Recreations of an Anthologist

Go and fetch a pint of Port
But let it not be such as that
You set before chance-comers,
But such whose father-grape grew fat
On Lusitanian summers.

ALFRED, LORD TENNYSON
English poet (1809-92)

Wines that, heaven knows when,
Had sucked the fire of some forgotten sun,
And kept it thro' a hundred years of gloom.

ALFRED, LORD TENNYSON: *The Golden Supper*

I give you one health in the juice of the vine,
The blood of the vineyard shall mingle with mine;
Thus let us drain the last dew drop of gold,
And empty our hearts of the blessings they hold.

OLIVER WENDALL HOLMES
American physician and writer (1809-94)

Wine. . . is a food.

OLIVER WENDELL HOLMES: *Address to Massachusetts Medical Society*

Come! fill a fresh bumper, for why should we go
While the nectar still reddens our cups as they flow.
Pour out the rich juices still bright with the sun,
'Till o'er the brimmed crystal the rubies shall run.

The purple globe clusters their life dews have bled;
How sweet is the breath of the fragrance they shed;
For summer's last roses lie hid in the wines
That were garnered by maidens who laughed through the vines.

Then a smile, and a glass, and a toast, and a cheer
For all the good wine, and we've some of it here!

OLIVER WENDELL HOLMES: *Ode for a Social Meeting*

Wine is the milk of the gods, milk the drink of babies, tea the drink of women, and water the drink of beasts.

JOHN STUART BLACKIE
Scottish scholar (1809-95)

Sip your spirits and cure your cold, but I will take port that will cure all things, even a bad character. For there was never a port drinker who lacked friends to speak for him.

WILLIAM MAKEPEACE THACKERAY
English novelist, essayist, and illustrator (1811-63)

The Bordeaux enlivens, the Burgundy invigorates; stronger drink only inflames; and where a bottle of good Beaune only causes a man to feel a certain manly warmth of benevolence—a glow something like that produced by sunshine and gentle exercise—a bottle of Chambertin will set all your frame in a fever, swell the extremities, and cause the pulses to throb.

WILLIAM MAKEPEACE THACKERAY: *Essays*

Grudge myself good wine? As soon grudge my horse corn.

WILLIAM MAKEPEACE THACKERAY

Fan the sinking flame of hilarity with the wing of friendship; and pass the rosy wine.

CHARLES DICKENS: *The Old Curiosity Shop*
English novelist (1812-70)

When the time grew near for retiring, Mr. Bounderby took a glass of water. "Oh, Sir!" said Mrs. Sparsit. "Not your sherry warm, with lemon-peel and nutmeg?" "Why, I have got out of the habit of taking it now, ma'am," said Mr. Bounderby. "The more's the pity, Sir," returned Mrs. Sparsit; "you are losing all your good old habits."

CHARLES DICKENS: *Hard Times*

Wine in moderation—not in excess, for that makes men ugly—has a thousand pleasant influences. It brightens the eye, improves the voice, imparts a new vivacity to one's thoughts and conversation.

CHARLES DICKENS: *Barnaby Rudge*

[Mr. Tulkinghorn] has a priceless binn of port in some artful cellar under the Fields, which is one of his many secrets. When he dines alone in chambers, he descends with a candle to the echoing regions below the deserted mansion, and, heralded by a remote reverberation of thundering doors, comes gravely back, encircled by an earthy atmosphere, and carrying a bottle from which he pours a radiant nectar, two score and ten years old, that blushes in the glass to find itself so famous, and fills the whole room with the fragrance of southern grapes.

CHARLES DICKENS: *Bleak House*

Champagne is one of the elegant extras of life.

CHARLES DICKENS

I proffer earth's product, not mine
Taste, try, and approve man's invention of—wine!
Illuminates gloom without sunny connivance,
Quaff wine,—how the spirits rise nimble and eager. . . .
The juice, I uphold,
Turns fear into hope and makes cowardice bold,—
Touching all that is leadlike in life turns it to gold!

> ROBERT BROWNING
> English poet (1812-89)

Rosy Wine

My Mistress' frowns are hard to bear,
And yet I will not quite despair;
Nor think, because her lips I leave,
There's nothing for me but to grieve.
—The goblet's lip awaiteth mine:
My grief I quench in rosy wine.

Dame Fortune too has faithless gone:
But let her go! I will not moan.
Draw in your chair, old Friend! and see
What rating Fortune has from me.
Clink yet again your glass with mine,—
To Fortune's health in rosy wine!

Pass, Fortune! pass, thou fickle jade!
One fortunately constant maid
Smiles on me yet; though loves depart,
Her presence gladdeneth my heart,
Thy tendrils cling, O loving Vine!
My griefs I quench in rosy wine.

> W. J. LINTON
> Anglo-American author (1812-98)

Red wine for children, champagne for men, and brandy for soldiers.

> OTTO VON BISMARCK
> Prusso-German statesman (1815-98)

Do you remember any great poet that ever illustrated the higher fields of humanity that did not dignify the use of wine from Homer on down?

> JAMES A. McDOUGALL
> United States senator (1817-67)

Bring me flesh and bring me wine,
Bring me pine logs hither.

> JOHN MASON NEALE: *Good King Wenceslas*
> English hymnologist (1818-66)

Better is old wine than new, and old friends likewise.

> CHARLES KINGSLEY: *Hereward the Wake*
> English author (1819-75)

WINE
DURING
MODERN
TIMES
(c. 1870 - present)

William
Stirling.

THE BEGINNING of the twentieth century was a dark period for the wine industry in the United States. The prohibition movement was in full swing, and anti-alcohol sentiment was rampant. On January 16, 1920, the eighteenth amendment went into effect, making it illegal for the general populace to produce, sell, or purchase alcoholic beverages in this country.

As a result, the American wine industry was ruined and hundreds of wineries were forced out of business. Only a few were able to survive by making medicinal wines or sacramental wines for religious ceremonies, both of which were still legal. Despite the fact that they no longer had wineries to sell to, the grape growers fared much better. A clause in the amendment allowed for the legal annual production of 200 gallons of wine in each home, and soon grapes became a very marketable commodity. California grape growers simply shipped their grapes across the continent to eastern markets for amateur winemakers.

Although California's production of grapes doubled during Prohibition, this was disastrous news for the wine industry. The grape varieties commonly used to make quality wines did not hold up well under the strenuous demands of cross-country shipping so, in order to survive, the grape growers tore up their existing vineyards and replanted them with sturdier varieties of grapes.

When Prohibition was finally repealed in 1933, the California vineyards were planted predominantly in these high-producing, low-quality grape varieties. In addition, a whole generation of winemakers had come and gone. Not only was it virtually impossible to find quality wine grapes in California, it was difficult to find qualified, experienced people to work in the wine industry. To further complicate the situation, the American public had to be re-educated about wine. The prestige which California wines had finally achieved in the late 1800s was destroyed. It would take decades to rebuild all that had been lost during those thirteen long, dark years of Prohibition.

The process of regeneration was a lengthy one. The Depression and World War II seriously deterred the growth of any new industry. Although approximately sixty new wineries opened in Napa Valley alone during the period immediately following Prohibition, the majority did not survive. Newcomers to the wine industry who were able to overcome the odds against them included The Christian Brothers, Louis M. Martini, and the Mondavis at Charles Krug. Those wineries who had made it through the "great experiment," such as Beaulieu, Inglenook, and Beringer, continued to persevere.

The 1950s were a period of revival for the American wine industry as post-war European immigration and American travel abroad encouraged people to become reacquainted with wine. New vineyards were planted and production increased. By 1963 Napa was once again recognized as the premier wine-producing region of the United States. Wines made during this period were largely mediocre, bulk-processed jug wines, but were popular and thereby served a vital purpose in re-introducing the American public to the world of wine.

In 1965 the first winery to be constructed in Napa since Prohibition marked the rebirth of the wine industry. Robert Mondavi left his family's winery of Charles Krug in St. Helena to establish his own down the road in Oakville. Mondavi was an innovative and demanding winemaker who emphasized the production of top-quality varietal wines. Experimenting with new technology, he constantly strived to find better ways to make better wines. His dedication and relentlessness inspired others, and soon additional "boutique" wineries were established throughout California. By 1975 there were over fifty wineries in the Napa Valley, and the American wine industry was back on its feet, once again producing quality wines.

One of the biggest achievements for the American wine industry during this century occurred in 1976 when American and French wines were sampled at a blind tasting held in Paris. Chateau Montelena garnered first place in the white burgundy category with its chardonnay, and a cabernet sauvignon from Stag's Leap Wine Cellars placed above the top French bordeaux. This coup did a great deal to enhance California's image as a producer of world-class wines, an image that continues to prevail as the wine industry grows and develops.

The past one hundred years of American wine history have come full circle, surviving the onslaught of two major catastrophes—disease brought on by Mother Nature and disease caused by humankind. Unfortunately, during the past few years both have once again become threats to the wine industry. While modern technology does battle with the latest influx of phylloxera, the human disease of "neo-prohibitionism" sweeps across the country. As Americans we must learn from our past mistakes and realize that the problem lies not with the product, but with people's attitudes. We must educate the public about the vital role wine has played in cultures historically throughout the world. The United States has sadly been lacking in this aspect. Wine has never been fully integrated into the American lifestyle, and, therefore, has never been treated with the reverence and respect its heritage so earnestly deserves. Only by incorporating wine into our culture and celebrating its rich traditions can we educate people, and deter the occasional misuse and abuse of this sacred beverage.

Education is currently underway with recent medical studies conducted at Harvard and in France showing wine to be a beneficial dietary supplement when consumed in moderate quantities. In fact, wine can help prevent the risk of heart disease by as much as fifty percent. Of course, this should not be astounding news. For thousands of years wine has been used as a therapeutic agent in cultures throughout the world. Perhaps we can learn something from our ancient ancestors by harkening back to the Greek poet, Alcaeus, who said simply, "Wine is the best medicine."

"Wine opens the heart."
"Opens it! It thaws it right out."
>HERMAN MELVILLE: *Confidence Man*
>American novelist (1819-91)

When wild with much thought, 'tis to wine I fly, to sober me.
>HERMAN MELVILLE: *Mardi*

The study of astronomy is wonderfully facilitated by wine.
>HERMAN MELVILLE: *Mardi*

Then fill the cup, fill high! fill high!
>Nor spare the rosy wine.
If death be in the cup, we'll die—
>Such death would be divine.
>>JAMES RUSSELL LOWELL: *To the Class of '38*
>>American poet, essayist, and diplomat (1819-91)

Though a sinner ye call me,
>I say it the same,—
Wine is nectar delicious,
>To scorn it a shame.
>>FRIEDRICH MARTIN VON BODENSTEDT
>>German writer (1819-92)

Drink not unfeelingly, nor yet unthinking drink!
Boast not too vauntingly, nor yet completely sink!
Where dazzling goblets shine, heed not the water ewer,—
He is not worthy wine who will not drink it pure!

In it the power lies to raise and to undo;
From out our goblets rise wisdom and folly, too.
But though in price of vine evil and good endure,—
He is not worthy wine who will not drink it pure!
>FRIEDRICH MARTIN VON BODENSTEDT

Pshaw, ye fools that talk of pleasure,
    Sitting by your goblets bright!
He must be a sage can measure
    Wine's ineffable delight!
        FRIEDRICH MARTIN VON BODENSTEDT

As the nightingale from rose-tree sips,
    Wise it is, and knows that it is good;
Thus with wine we damp our rosy lips,—
    Wise are we, and know that it is good.

Like a spectre-king that unseen trips
    From the depths of some far-honey'd wood,
Wine should pass the rose-gate of our lips,—
    Wise are we, and know that it is good.
        FRIEDRICH MARTIN VON BODENSTEDT

A dose of brandy, by stimulating the circulation, produces
Dutch courage.
        HERBERT SPENCER: *The Study of Sociology*
        English philosopher, journalist, and writer (1820-1903)

Within the bottle's depths, the wine's soul sang one night.
        CHARLES BAUDELAIRE
        French poet and critic (1821-67)

Champagne with its amber hue, its eclat, its sparkle and its
perfume arouses the senses and produces a cheerfulness
which flashes through the company like a spark of electricity.
At the magic word champagne the guests, dull and torpid
with good feeding, awake at once. This lively, ethereal and
charming beverage sets in motion the spirits of all; the phleg-
matic, the grave and the philosophic are surprised to find
themselves amiable; in the wink of an eye (or the pop of a cork)
the whole banquet has changed its physiognomy.
        CHARLES BAUDELAIRE

I sometimes think I hear wine talking. It speaks with its soul, with that spiritual voice which is only heard by the spirit: "Man, my beloved, from within my prison of glass locked with cork I yearn to sing you a song full of brotherhood, a song full of joy and light and expectation. I am not ungrateful; I know I owe this life to you. I know it has cost you labor with the sun beating down on your shoulders. You have given me life, and I shall recompense you. Generously shall I repay my debt, for I experience an enormous joy when I tumble down a work-parched throat. An honest man's chest is a resting place that pleases me much more than these melancholy and feeling cellars. It is a joyous tomb where I fulfill my destiny with enthusiasm. I create a prodigious flurry in the worker's stomach and from there by invisible staircases I climb to his brain where I perform my supreme dance. Do you hear stirring and re-echoing mighty choruses of ancient times in me, songs of love and glory? I am the soul of your homeland, part troubadour and part soldier. The hope of Sundays am I. Work makes for prosperous weekdays, wine for happy Sundays. With your sleeves rolled up and your elbows on the family table, you will glory in me proudly and you will be truly content."

CHARLES BAUDELAIRE: *An Essay on Wine*

GET DRUNK

One must always be drunk. Everything is there: It is the essential issue. To avoid that horrible burden of Time grabbing your shoulders and crushing you to the earth, you must get drunk without restraint.

But on what? On wine, poetry or virtue, whatever you fancy. But get drunk.

If sometimes, on palace walks, in the green grass of a ditch or the gloomy solitude of your room, you wake, and find that drunkenness is wearing off, ask the wind, the wave, the star, the bird, the clock, everything that flees, that laments, that turns, that sings, that speaks, ask what time it is; and the wind, the wave, the star, the bird, and the clock will answer you: "It is time to get drunk." To escape being the martyred slaves of time, be continually drunk. On wine, poetry or virtue, whatever you fancy.

CHARLES BAUDELAIRE

Wine is the most healthful and most hygienic of beverages.

LOUIS PASTEUR
French chemist and microbiologist (1822-95)

The flavor of wine is like delicate poetry.

LOUIS PASTEUR

Wine—bring wine—
Flushing high with its growth divine,
In the crystal depth of my soul to shine;
Whose glow was caught
From the warmth which Fancy's summer brought
From the vintage fields in the Land of Thought.

BAYARD TAYLOR
American writer (1825-78)

Day and night my thoughts incline
to the blandishments of wine,
Jars were made to drain, I think;
Wine, I know, was made to drink.

R. H. STODDARD
American poet and literary critic (1825-1903)

When I die—the day be far!
Should the potters make a jar
Out of this poor clay of mine,
Let the jar be filled with wine!

R. H. STODDARD

A house with a great wine stored below lives in our imaginations as a joyful house, fast and splendidly rooted in the soil.

> GEORGE MEREDITH: *The Egoist*
> English novelist and poet (1828-1909)

Hocks, too, have compassed age. I have tasted senior hocks. Their flavours are as a brook of many voices: they have depth also. Senatorial Port! we say. We cannot say that of any other wine. Port is deep-sea deep. It is in its flavour deep; mark the difference. It is like a classic tragedy, organic in conception. An ancient Hermitage has the light of the antique; the merit that it can grow to an extreme old age; a merit. Neither of Hermitage or of Hock can you say that it is the blood of those long years, retaining the strength of youth with the wisdom of age. To Port for that! Port is our noblest legacy! Observe, I do not compare the wines: I distinguish the qualities. Let them live together for our enrichment; they are not rivals like the Idean three. Were they rivals, a fourth would challenge them. Burgundy has great genius. It does wonders within its period; it does all except to keep up in the race; it is short lived. An aged Burgundy runs with a beardless Port. I cherish the fancy that Port speaks the sentences of wisdom. Burgundy sings the inspired ode. Or put it, that Port is the Homeric hexameter, Burgundy the Pindaric dithyramb. . . . Pindar astounds. But his elder brings us the more sustaining cup. One is a fountain of prodigious ascent. One is the unsounded purple sea of marching billows.

> GEORGE MEREDITH: *The Egoist*

There's no law possible without wine. Law is an occupation which dries the blood.

> GEORGE MEREDITH: *Ordeal of Richard Feverel*

Thy sacred emblems to partake—
Thy consecrated bread to take
And thine immortal wine!

> EMILY DICKINSON: *No. 130*
> American poet (1830-86)

While there's life on the lips,
   while there's warmth in the wine;
One deep health do I pledge,
   and that health shall be thine.

OWEN MEREDITH
English statesman and poet (1831-91)

"Have some wine," the March Hare said in an encouraging tone. Alice looked all round the table, but there was nothing on it but tea.
"I don't see any wine," she remarked.
"There isn't any," said the March Hare.
"Then it wasn't very civil of you to offer it," said Alice angrily.

LEWIS CARROLL: *Alice's Adventures in Wonderland*
English logician and novelist (1832-98)

But the monarch of all wines is Champagne. Ah, me! How it bubbles, how it sparkles, this most ravishing of all wines! It is at once the most enticing, and the most exhilarating. It is genial, comforting, stimulating, irradiating and divine. It refreshes, regales, cheers and transports.

MAJOR BENJAMIN CUMMINGS TRUMAN: *See How It Sparkles*
American journalist and author (1835-1916)

Wine is like rain: when it falls on the mire it but makes it the fouler, But when it strikes the good soil wakes it to beauty and bloom.

JOHN HAY: *Distichs*
American statesman and writer (1838-1905)

Pass me the wine. To those that keep
The bachelor's secluded sleep,
Peaceful, inviolate, and deep,
   I pour libation.

HENRY AUSTIN DOBSON
English poet (1840-1921)

No other wine produces an equal effect in increasing the success of a party, and a judicious Champagne-giver is sure to win the goodwill and respect even of those who can command it at pleasure.

THOMAS WALKER
American art collector (1840-1928)

One not only drinks wine, one smells it, observes it, tastes it, sips it and—one talks about it.

KING EDWARD VII
English monarch (1841-1910)

Wine, madam, is God's next best gift to man.

AMBROSE BIERCE: *The Devil's Dictionary*
American journalist and author (1842-1914)

If Claret is the queen of natural wines, Burgundy is the king.

GEORGE SAINTSBURY: *Notes on a Cellar-Book*
English literary critic, journalist, and educator
(1845-1933)

[Port] strengthens while it gladdens as no other wine can do.

GEORGE SAINTSBURY: *Notes on a Cellar-Book*

When [the wines] were good they pleased my senses, cheered my spirits, improved my moral and intellectual powers, besides enabling me to confer the same benefits on other people.

GEORGE SAINTSBURY: *Notes on a Cellar-Book*

It is sometimes forgotten that only one of the two peaks of Parnassus was sacred to Apollo, the other belonging to Dionysus.

GEORGE SAINTSBURY: *Notes on a Cellar-Book*

T<small>HE</small> S<small>PIRIT OF</small> W<small>INE</small>

The Spirit of Wine
Sang in my glass, and I listened
With love to his odorous music,
His flushed and magnificent song.
—'I am health, I am heart, I am life!
For I give for the asking
The fire of my father, the Sun,
And the strength of my mother, the Earth.

Inspiration in essence,
I am wisdom and wit to the wise,
His visible muse to the poet,
The soul of desire to the lover,
The genius of laughter to all.

'Come lean on me, ye that are weary!
Rise, ye faint-hearted and doubting!
Haste, ye that lag by the way!
I am Pride, the consoler;
Valor and Hope are my henchmen;
I am the Angel of Rest.

'I am life, I am wealth, I am fame:
For I captain an army
Of shining and generous dreams;
And mine, too, all mine, are the keys
Of that secret spiritual shrine,
Where, his work-a-day soul put by,
Shut in with his saint of saints—
With his radiant and conquering self—
Man worships, and talks, and is glad.

'Come, sit with me, ye that are lonely,
Ye that are paid with disdain,
Ye that are chained and would soar!
I am beauty and love;
I am friendship, the comforter;
I am that which forgives and forgets.'—

The Spirit of Wine
Sang in my heart, and I triumphed
In the savour and scent of his music,
His magnetic and mastering song.

> WILLIAM ERNEST HENLEY
> English poet, critic, playwright, and editor (1849-1903)

A bottle of good wine, like a good act, shines ever in the retrospect.

> ROBERT LOUIS STEVENSON: *Napa Wine*
> Scottish author and critic (1850-94)

Wine of California. . . inimitable fragrance and soft fire. . . and the wine is bottled poetry.

> ROBERT LOUIS STEVENSON: *Silverado Squatters*

Now then, the songs; but first, more wine.
The gods be with you, friends of mine!

> EUGENE FIELD
> American writer (1850-95)

There is a glorious candor in an honest quart of wine,
A certain inspiration which I cannot well define.
How it bubbles, how it sparkles, how its gurgling seems to say:
"Come! on a tide of rapture let me float your soul away!"

> EUGENE FIELD

Now and then it is a joy to have one's table red with wine and roses.

> OSCAR WILDE: *De Profundis*
> Irish poet, wit, and dramatist (1854-1900)

Wine, therefore, is considered on two distinct grounds as a spirit, or containing a spirit; first because as a red juice, it is identified with the blood of the plant, and second because it intoxicates or inspires.

> JAMES GEORGE FRAZER: *The Golden Bough*
> British social anthropologist and folklorist (1854-1941)

I'm only a beer teetotaller, not a champagne teetotaller.

> GEORGE BERNARD SHAW: *Candida*
> Irish essayist, dramatist, critic, and pamphleteer (1856-1950)

As the vintages of earth
Taste of the sun that riped their birth,
We know that never cadent Sun
Thy lamped clusters throbbed upon,
What plumed feet the winepress trod;
Thy wine is flavorous of God.

> FRANCIS THOMPSON
> English poet (1859-1907)

A glass of wine filled to the brim,
Does much more than Milton can
To justify the ways of God to man.

> A. E. HOUSMAN
> English poet, essayist, and scholar (1859-1936)

Bouquet is the soul of the wine, while an agreeable aroma unfailingly imparts a delicious sensation.

> FRONA EUNICE WAIT: *Wines and Vines of California*
> American journalist and writer (1859-1946)

Although man is already ninety per cent water, the Prohibitionists are not yet satisfied.

> JOHN KENDRICK BANGS
> American humorist (1862-1922)

Here's to old Adam's crystal ale,
  Clear, sparkling, and divine,
Fair H$_2$O, long may you flow,
  We drink your health (in wine).

> OLIVER HERFORD
> English writer and illustrator (1863-1935)

Here's to mine and here's to thine!
  Now's the time to clink it!
Here's a flagon of old wine,
  And here we are to drink it.

> RICHARD HOVEY
> American poet (1864-1900)

For love and song
  To the vine belong,
To the vine, with its strength Titanic;
  Small wonder it grows
  Where the lava flows,
And the warm earth heaves volcanic.

From the East it came
  With its warmth of flame,
And the Orient gave it fire;
  Then sang the vine
  In Palestine,
And they trod the grape at Tyre.

And the prophet and seer
  Of old Judea,
With the wise of all the ages,
  Have sung of wine
  In strains divine,
From Papyrus to printed pages.

What was praised by them
  Shall our lips condemn?

From such cant may the Lord deliver!
    Let heart be merry,
    God gave his berry,
And God is a careful giver!
>JOSEPH DANA MILLER
>American writer (1864-1939)

You Americans have the loveliest wines in the world, you know, but you don't realize it. You call them "domestic" and that's enough to start trouble anywhere.
>H. G. WELLS
>British writer and social reformer (1866-1946)

The sixtieth cup makes me wise with wine,
A thousand riddles clear as crystal shine;
And much I wonder what it can have been
That used to puzzle this poor head of mine.
Yet with the morn the wine-deserted brain
Sees all its riddles trooping back again:—
Say, am I sober when I see naught clear?
And am I drunk when I see all things plain?
>RICHARD LE GALLIENNE
>English writer (1866-1947)

All wines are by their very nature full of reminiscence, the golden tears and red blood of summers that are gone.
>RICHARD LE GALLIENNE

There are no sorrows wine cannot allay,
There are no sins wine cannot wash away,
There are no riddles wine knows not to read,
There are no debts wine is too poor to pay.
>RICHARD LE GALLIENNE

They are not long, the days of wine and roses;
Out of a misty dream
Our path emerges for awhile, then closes
Within a dream.

ERNEST DOWSON: *Vitae Summa Brevis*
English poet (1867-1900)

[W]ine is the professor of taste, the liberator of the spirit, and
the light of intelligence.

PAUL CLAUDEL
French diplomat, poet, and drama critic (1868-1955)

Gentle friends, forbear to laugh
As I toast the wine I quaff—
Scarce the wisdom Omar found
All its beauty can expound;
As its happy lover sips,
All its fragrance haunts his lips,
All its warmth along the veins
Flowing from the cup he drains;
All its brightness his enhances
As it sparkles in his glances,
All its kindliness awhile
Lingering upon his smile.
Fair companions, what can be
Truer friend to you and me?
Love his troth may soon dissever,—
Wine gives all, and gives forever.

GEORGE STERLING
American poet (1869-1926)

He who clinks his cup with mine,
Adds a glory to the wine.

GEORGE STERLING

To exalt, enthrone, establish and defend,
To welcome home mankind's mysterious friend:
Wine, true begetter of all arts that be;
Wine, privilege of the completely free;
Wine the recorder; wine the sagely strong;
Wine, bright avenger of sly-dealing wrong,
Awake, Ausonian Muse, and sing the vineyard song!

HILAIRE BELLOC: *Heroic Poem in Praise of Wine*
Anglo-French writer and poet (1870-1953)

But, Ah! With Orvieto, with that name
Of dark, Etrurian, subterranean flame
The years dissolve. I am standing in that hour
Of majesty Septembral, and the power
Which swells the clusters when the nights are still
With autumn stars on Orvieto hill.

HILAIRE BELLOC: *Heroic Poem in Praise of Wine*

Comrade-Commander whom I dared not earn,
What said You then to trembling friends and few?
'A moment, and I drink it with you new:
But in my Father's Kingdom.' So, my Friend.
Let not Your cup desert me in the end.
But when the hour of mine adventure's near
Just and benignant, let my youth appear
Bearing a Chalice, open, golden, wide,
With benediction graven on its side.
So touch my dying lip: so bridge that deep:
So pledge my waking from the gift of sleep,
And, sacramental, raise me the Divine:
Strong brother in God and last companion, Wine.

HILAIRE BELLOC: *Heroic Poem in Praise of Wine*

It is true that taste can be educated. It is also true that taste can
be perverted. . . . If any man gives you a wine you can't bear,
don't say it is beastly. . . but don't say you like it. You are
endangering your soul and the use of wine as well. Seek out
some other wine good to your taste.

HILAIRE BELLOC

155

A Grace After Drink

Oh, hear us, kindly Bacchus,
　　Lord of good revelry,
Whose bright elixir teacheth men
　　What the mortals be—

When next thy joyous satyrs
　　Make revelry divine,
And blend in early spring the sap
　　That mellows into wine,

Grant that they mix no malice,
　　Nor sudden fray, nor strife,
Nor black despond nor evil thought,
　　Nor dull despair of life,

But only wit and kindness,
　　And laughter fair and strong,
And sweet content and merriment
　　That move the heart to song!

So, when the grapes are bursting
　　Along thy favored hills,
And through the frozen veins of men
　　Thy golden summer thrills,

Grant, then, that we, thy servants,
　　Shall drink in soberness,
And hold thy godly gift too dear
　　For barb'rous gross excess.

And aye from every flagon
　　The maiden draught be thine—
A toast to merry Bacchus,
　　Lord giver of the vine!
　　　　Will Irwin
　　　　American journalist and writer (1873-1948)

156

I was very well brought up. As a first proof of so categorical a statement, I shall simply say that I was no more than three years old when my father poured out my first full liquer glass of an amber-colored wine which was sent up to him from the Midi, where he was born: the muscat of Frontignan.

The sun breaking from behind clouds, a shock of sensuous pleasure, an illumination of my newborn tastebuds! This initiation ceremony rendered me worthy of wine for all time. A little later I learned to empty my goblet of mulled wine, scented with cinnamon and lemon, as I ate a dinner of boiled chestnuts. At an age when I could still scarcely read, I was spelling out, drop by drop, old light clarets and dazzling Yquems. Champagne appeared in its turn, a murmur of foam, leaping pearls of air providing an accompaniment to birthday and First Communion banquets, complementing the gray truffles from La Puisaye. . . . Good lessons from which I graduated to a familiar and discreet use of wine, not gulped down greedily but measured out into narrow glasses, assimilated mouthful by spaced-out, meditative mouthful.

It was between my eleventh and fifteenth years that this admirable educational program was perfected. My mother was afraid that I was outgrowing my strength and was in danger of a "decline." One by one, she unearthed, from their bed of dry sand, certain bottles that had been aging beneath our house in a cellar—which is, thanks be to God, still intact—hewn out of fine, solid granite. I feel envious, when I think back, of the privileged little urchin I was in those days. As an accompaniment to my modest, fill-in meals—a chop, a leg of cold chicken, or one of those hard cheeses, "baked" in the embers of a wood fire and so brittle that one blow of the fist would shatter them into pieces like a pane of glass—I drank Chateau Lafites, Chambertins, and Cortons which had escaped capture by the "Prussians" in 1870. Certain of these wines were already fading, pale and scented still like a dead rose; they lay on a sediment of tannin that darkened their bottles, but most of them retained their aristocratic ardor and their invigorating powers. The good old days!

I drained that paternal cellar, goblet by goblet, delicately. . . . My mother would recork the bottle and contemplate the glory of the great French vineyards in my cheeks.

Happy those children who are not made to blow out their stomachs with great glasses of red-tinted water during their meals! Wise those parents who measure out to their progeny a tiny glass of pure wine—and I mean "pure" in the noble sense of the word—and teach them: "Away from the meal table you have the pump, the faucet, the spring, and the filter at your disposal. Water is for quenching the thirst. Wine, according to its quality and the soil where it was grown, is a necessary tonic, a luxury, and a fitting tribute to good food." And is it not also a source of nourishment in itself? Yes, those were the days, when a few true natives of my Burgundy village, gathered around a flagon swathed in dust and spiders' webs, kissing the tips of their fingers from their lips, exclaimed—already—"a nectar!"

COLETTE: *Wines*
French novelist (1873-1954)

The vine and the wine it produces are two great mysteries. Alone in the vegetable kingdom, the vine makes the true savor of the earth intelligible to man. With what fidelity it makes the translation! It senses, then expresses, in its clusters of fruit the secrets of the soil. The flint, through the vine, tells us that it is living, fusible, a giver of nourishment. Only in wine does the ungrateful chalk pour out its golden tears. A vine, transported across mountains and over seas, will struggle to keep its personality, and sometimes triumphs over the powerful chemistries of the mineral world. Harvested near Algiers, a white wine will still remember without fail, year after year, the noble Bordeaux graft that gave it exactly the right hint of sweetness, lightened its body, and endowed it with gaiety. And it is far-off Jerez that gives its warmth and color to the dry and cordial wine that ripens at Chateau Chalon, on the summit of a narrow, rocky plateau.

COLETTE: *Wines*

Lily on liquid roses floating—
So floats yon foam o'er pink champagne:
Fain would I join such pleasant boating,
And prove that ruby main,
And float away on wine!

> JOHN KENYON: *Champagne Rosee*
> American phonetician and professor (1874-1959)

And Noah he often said to his wife when he sat down to dine,
'I don't care where the water goes if it doesn't get into the wine.

> G. K. CHESTERTON: *Wine and Water*
> English critic, novelist, and poet (1874-1936)

Feast on wine or fast on water
And your honor shall stand sure,
God Almighty's son and daughter,
He the valiant, she the pure!

> G. K. CHESTERTON

The wine they drink in Paradise
They make in Haute Lorraine.

> G. K. CHESTERTON: *A Cider Song*

A good party is where you enjoy good people, and they taste
even better with champagne.

> WILSON MIZNER
> American architect and developer (1876-1933)

Wine in itself is an excellent thing.

> POPE PIUS XII
> Pope of Roman Catholic Church (1876-1958)

Wine is, indeed, a living thing, brash in its youth, full-blossoming in its maturity, but subject, if not used in time, to senility, decay, and death.

ANDRE L. SIMON
French wine writer (1877-1970)

Sherry is the brightest jewel in the vinous crown of Spain. There is no wine like it.

ANDRE L. SIMON

From the earliest times down to the seventeenth century all civilized men drank wine whenever they could procure it. They did not drink wine because they had nothing else to drink, nor because wine was more pleasing to the taste. They had ale, mead, and all sorts of honey drinks which probably contained as much alcohol as wine and being so much sweeter, were more pleasant to less educated palates. But it was wine that they sought, always, instinctively, whether it was easy to procure or not, whether it was really good or not. They do not seem to have cared for wine on account of its taste nearly so much as on account of the good which they knew, from tradition and their own personal experience, that they derived from its use.

ANDRE L. SIMON: *Wine and the Wine-Trade*

Wine is the suitably fermented juice of the grape. Wine is the living blood of the grape. Wine is the most wholesome and beneficial beverage, one that is beyond compare as regards the antiquity, the ubiquity and the catholicity of its appeal.

ANDRE L. SIMON: *Wine and the Wine-Trade*

The joy that is in Wine is the joy of sunshine. It has nothing in common with the dentist's laughing gas. It has nothing in common with many of the drugs and poisons which so many people crave for in their search for peace of

160

mind and nerves. Wine is not a drug. It is never a craving. It seldom becomes even a mere habit. It is an instinct, man's time-honoured urge to joy.

ANDRE L. SIMON: *Wine and the Wine-Trade*

Wine enhances every meal ... but to the French, wine enhances life itself.

ANDRE L. SIMON: *The Commonsense of Wine*

Wine makes every meal an occasion, every table more elegant, every day more civilized.

ANDRE L. SIMON: *The Commonsense of Wine*

Meals are an inescapable necessity, but they must never be allowed to become dull, monotonous, a chore instead of the tonic and the joy that they should be and can so easily be. Pleasant company at mealtime makes all the difference, and there is pleasant company to be had for the asking—and a few coins—in a bottle of good wine on the table.

Food that is partnered with the right wine tastes better, we enjoy it more, it is digested better and it does us more good. No meal is ever dull when there is wine to drink and talk about.

ANDRE L. SIMON: *The Commonsense of Wine*

Wine the consoler, the friend, the joyful companion for those who receive it in all gratitude and humility.

ANDRE L. SIMON: *Drink*

And all through the term of his life, man has much to learn, much to bear and suffer—trials, doubts, injustice, failures— but he also has much to help—faith, friendship, success and the tonic that is wine. Wine is to the parched mind of man what water is to the sun-drenched plain. It releases the brakes of his self-consciousness and softens the hard-baked crust of dust so that the seeds below may send forth sweet flowers.

ANDRE L. SIMON: *Drink*

[Wine] helps us to penetrate the veil; it gives us glimpses of the Magi of creation where they sit weaving their spells and sowing their seeds of incantation to the flowing mind.

DON MARQUIS: *The Almost Perfect State*
American journalist and humorist (1878-1937)

What comtemptible scoundrel stole the cork from my lunch?

W. C. FIELDS
American actor and comedian (1880-1946)

Penicillin cures, but wine makes people happy.

SIR ALEXANDER FLEMING
English bacteriologist (1881-1955)

[The magnum of 1864 Chateau Lafite] was like passing from fine prose to the inspiration of poetry.

H. WARNER ALLEN: *The Wines of France*
(b. 1881)

Great wine is a work of art. It produces a harmony of pleasing sensations, which appeal directly to the aesthetic sense, and at the same time sharpens the wit, gladdens the heart, and stimulates all that is most generous in human nature. Its proper appreciation is difficult and complicated, and demands a certain education on the part of the drinker. For in that appreciation the three senses of sight, smell, and taste are all concerned, and the impressions which it causes are exceedingly delicate in their multiplicity and almost defy analysis. Moreover wine is a living thing, not a mere chemical composition; like any living organism, it is young, grows old, and eventually decays and dies, the cycle of its life depending on that of the fermentation microbes which bestow on it its nature and excellence.

H. WARNER ALLEN: *The Wines of France*

There is a free masonry among wine-lovers. In that goodly fellowship the man who by some divine chance has unearthed a rare and precious bottle is at once preoccupied with an anxious thought: he feels that he owes it to a noble wine to share it with some other wine-lover worthy to enjoy its quality and able to discuss its particular merits. Selfishness is a vice unknown to the wine-lover.

H. WARNER ALLEN: *Viniana*

Its [Chateau Margaux 1871] magic bouquet envelops the senses in a cloud of airy fragrance, scented like the breezes from the Islands of the Blest, a dream of grace and delicacy, the twinkling feet of dancing nymphs set free in our tedious world. Its subtle symphony of ever-varied shades of beauty partakes of the poetry of speed, of the perfect lines that form and break and form again as dancers weave an agile pattern.

H. WARNER ALLEN: *A History of Wine*

The 'Open Sesame' of a love of wine exercises something akin to the magic power of local patriotism to unite its votaries in friendship and a masonry with no secrets in which every novice is greeted as one who will by sharing and appreciating increase the value of the treasure possessed by those more fortunate and experienced. The possessor of precious bottles will not draw their corks, until he has gathered a circle of friends capable of making the most of their potential beauties.

H. WARNER ALLEN: *A History of Wine*

Port is essentially the wine of philosophical contemplation.

H. WARNER ALLEN: *The Romance of Wine*

Wine-lovers are unselfish folk. Few if any of them care to drink their choicest wine when they are alone. For that experience loses half its fascination if it is not accompanied by the conversation of good fellowship and that discussion of the wine, which carries its memory to the gods by apt comparisons and seasoned praise based on the remembrance of other wines. I have heard of egotists who sought to buy up all the bottles that remained of some rare vintage that they might have the satisfaction of knowing that no other oenologist, no other connoisseur, could set it on his table, but even then their selfishness was concerned not with the greediness of drinking it themselves, but with the more generous vanity of offering it to their friends.

H. WARNER ALLEN: *The Romance of Wine*

The wines that one remembers best are not necessarily the finest that one has tasted, and the highest quality may fail to delight so much as some far more humble beverage drunk in more favourable surroundings.

H. WARNER ALLEN: *A Contemplation of Wine*

CHAMPAGNE

Lulled in a nine year's sleep
A child of Dionysus here abides
Imprisoned in his keep
Of dark green glass with round and glassy sides,
The entrance stopped with a cork and metal cap
And muzzled like a dog with cage of wire—
Grim skeleton bedizened in a wrap
Of golden foil like kingly shroud that hides
Disintegration in a proud attire.
But loose the wire, and, lo, the prisoned slave
Stretches his muscles, heaves at the tight-closed door,
Heaves yet again and, like the whispering wave
That bursts frost-sparkling on a summer shore,
Leaps out, a fount of foam; then, changed again,
Dissolves to liquid sunlight. Golden wine
Brims every glass. Seen through each crystal pane,
In tall straight jets or whirled in spiral twine
The hurrying air-beads to the surface strain,
An April shower of bright inverted rain.

MARTIN ARMSTRONG
English poet and writer (b. 1882)

Hock

Turn eastward, Bacchus: it is time to go
From Burgundy, Champagne, Cognac, Bordeaux,
Across the frontier. Here we shall replenish
Our empty cups with that pale amber Rhenish
Pressed from the clusters of your sacred vine
That clothes the hills of many-castled Rhine.
Choose well the route, for we must visit first
Rheinhessen, there to halt and quench our thirst
With Nierstein and the names of lesser breed
Whose limpid charm shall answer to our need
After the dusty march to Germany.
But when our weary Maenads, putting by
The proffered cup, for richer draughts shall cry,
We'll turn aside their lickerish lust to sate
With odorous wines of the Palatinate
Whose short-lived beauty sickens and is dead
Ere nobler wines their callow youth have shed.
But we who tirelessly pursue the best
Must northward march to where the stream flows west
To Rheingau hills whose far-famed vineyards climb
From Hochheim on the Main to Rudesheim.
There in the shadow of some castled rock
We'll stretch at ease and sip the best of Hock,
Determining with learned tongue and nose
Whether the honeysuckle or the rose
Apes best these subtle essences that run
Through Nineteen Twenty and Nineteen Twenty One.

MARTIN ARMSTRONG

Burgundy

Praise now the ancient Duchy of the Vine
Where the warm tide of summer sunlight spills
On vineyards ranged along the Golden Hills,
Upbrimming every long and leafy line.

In grapes of Chambertin and Clos de Beze,
Richebourg, La Romanee, lie darkly curled

The purple kings of all the vinous world;
Till from the dusky fruit in autumn days

That juice is crushed which slowly, subtlely grows,
Through hidden workings, whispered fermentations,
Like ghostly dancers mixed in strange mutations,
To essence of the ruby and the rose.

Be patient then, while generous years devise
Maturity and riches to the wine,
Till, to perfection come, it darkly shine
Upon the banquets of the truly wise.

MARTIN ARMSTRONG

Rare Vintages and Vin Ordinaire

These are the children of long years of peace,
The high nobility of earth's increase,
    Superbly useless, set apart.
A symbol and epitome of art.
Not theirs the genial office to assuage
The labourer's thirst, but solely to engage
Sophisticated palates and invite
To feasts of intellectual delight.
In famous vineyards of the white or red
Meticulously tended, pruned and fed,
Gathered and pressed and to the vats conveyed
They wait in comfortable darkness laid
    (Potential riches held in trust)
The gradual fermentation of the must,
Till, in due season grown authentic wine
By process scientific and divine,
Locked in their glassy cells they shall begin
The long novitiate of the Chateau bin.
Raised to the priesthood each, an anchoret
Cloistered in crystal, lies imprisoned yet,
For not to such as these shall come the call
Till robed and hatted as a Cardinal.
But these are matters more than half divine.

166

Now let us praise the wine
That quenched the thirst of Chaucer, Rabelais,
Ronsard and Shakespeare, wine of every day
That warms the blood and strengthens talk and cheer
With wholesome draughts born of no boasted year,
Pressed in no vaunted vineyard, with no name
To catch the eye and set the thoughts aflame;
 Of mere generic stock
 Yet potent to unlock
The wagging tongue of Falstaff and entrance
The Spanish Knight of doleful countenance,
 And wash the monstrous away
 Of Patriarch Grangrousier.
Let none of us contemptuously rebuff
 Wine that was good enough
For men like these, but gladly sit and share
Our honest, rough, refreshing Ordinaire.

   MARTIN ARMSTRONG

Suns that matured the vines of old
 And vanished in the winter rain,
Here in their bright essential gold
 Await your lips to dawn again.

Inhale and sip, and you'll remember
 And back to living beauty bring
The sharp and sweet of late September,
 The cool bouquet of early spring.

A fragrance caught from flowers that perished,
 Old suns called back to light, that shone
On vineyards by the warm South cherished
 Above the waters of Garonne;

Vineyards whose names come blandly smiling
 Like Bacchanals on dancing toe,
The palate of the mind beguiling,—
 Climens, Couet, Fargues, Filhot.

   MARTIN ARMSTRONG: *Golden Sauternes*

Through centuries unnumbered men of old
Broke stubborn earth and taught the trailing Vine
And trod the bubbling press and drank the Wine,
Contented with the Ruby and the Gold;
Till someone of a subtler essence dreamed
And poured the wine into a copper still
And set a gradual fire beneath, until
Eddies of odorous mist arose and steamed
Along a curling Pipe, condensed, and streamed
In trickling drops into a chamber cool
And mounted slowly in a luscious pool
In whose dim eye a sullen topaz gleamed.
Then in an oaken Cask of portly shape
He stored the subtle spirit and darkly smiled,
Knowing that he had craftily beguiled
The Essence of the Essence of the Grape.

MARTIN ARMSTRONG: *Brandy*

P<small>ORT</small>

In Vintage Port of noble year
What multifarious joys appear—
A liquid ruby; a bouquet
Like odours of a tropic day,
So ripe you'd almost say it glows
In the portals of the nose;
A palate luscious yet serene,
The right essential Hippocrene,
Blandness combined with potency;
A finish dry, but not too dry,
With just a hint of cedarwood
To spice the ripe fruit's nectarous blood.

Certain pundits, here unnamed,
Have unequivocally claimed
That '63 and '68
Could turn the hinges of Heaven's Gate:
Some have held that '87

Rose to not so far from Heaven,
While others resolutely stated
That '87 was overrated,
'90 caught it up and beat it.
But if we gathered and repeated
All that has been written, said,
Argued, thought, upon this head,
And set ourselves to celebrate
Younger wines by name and date,
We should drift—a fact that shocks
By its glaring paradox—
On and on in such a sort
As never to get home to Port.

MARTIN ARMSTRONG

CLARET

What brain can fitly shape
A song to praise this grape,
Ranked over hill and plain
In lands about Bordeaux
Where the three rivers flow
To join the Atlantic main?

Praise first the great Chateaux
Lafite, Latour, Margaux,
Then two scarce less than these—
Haut-Brion and Ausone,
Then all those names well known
Of wines of all degrees.

From St Estephe, Pauillac,
St Julien, Cantenac,
And from the river isles;
For never wine that grows
Palate and eye and nose
So delicately beguiles.

Then thank we God the giver
Of sun and soil and river
And that ancestral root
Set in the midst to muster
Green leaf and flower and cluster
Of ruby-hearted fruit.

MARTIN ARMSTRONG

What is better than to sit at the end of the day and drink wine with friends, or substitutes for friends?

JAMES JOYCE: *quoted by Richard Ellman in biography*
Irish writer (1882-1941)

My only regret in life is that I did not drink more champagne.

JOHN MAYNARD KEYNES
English economist (1883-1946)

[The wine] was golden in colour, suave and yet virile, as if a breeze of the sea had swept the grape and the ghost of its tang still clung and mingled with the bloom.

D. B. WYNDHAM LEWIS: *On Straw and Other Conceits*
English artist, writer, and critic (1884-1957)

Our pale day is sinking into twilight,
And if we sip the wine, we find dreams coming upon us
Out of the imminent night.

D. H. LAWRENCE: *Grapes*
English poet and novelist (1885-1930)

New loves and old wines:
Give a man these and he never repines.

FRANCIS BEEDING: *Heads Off at Midnight*
English drama critic and novelist (1885-1944)

And one can always be very careful if one just has a little glass of bubbly along with one's predicament.

ISAK DINESEN
Danish writer (1885-1962)

What is man when you come to think on him, but a minutely set, ingenious machine for turning, with infinite artfulness, the red wine of Shiraz into urine?

ISAK DINESEN: SEVEN GOTHIC TALES

The great thing about making cognac is that it teaches you above everything else to wait—man proposes, but time and God and the seasons have got to be on your side.

JEAN MONNET
French statesman (1888-1979)

Religions change: beer and wine remain.

HERVEY ALLEN: *Anthony Adverse*
American author (1889-1949)

Anyone who knows history. . . must surely know his wines.

ARNOLD TOYNBEE
English historian (1889-1975)

Wine has been to me a firm friend and a wise counsellor. Often, wine has shown me matters in their true perspective, and has, as though by the touch of a magic wand, reduced great disasters to small inconveniences. Wine has lit up for me the pages of literature, and revealed in life romance lurking in the commonplace.

ALFRED DUFF COOPER
British statesman and author (1890-1954)

You can have too much champagne to drink, but you can never

have enough.

ELMER RICE: *The Winner*
American dramatist (1892-1967)

IVRESSE

Fill the glass and let me drink
to purposeless delight
that mocks the sacred and profane of life.
Fill the glass and let me taste
the magic journey, wine,
that finds a road to heaven
through any pain.

Fill the glass and let me drink
the pungent fires of hell
while Death himself toasts in return
to my Good Health!

MATTEOS ZARIFIAN
Armenian poet (1894-1924)

It's a naive domestic Burgundy without any breeding, but I
believe you'll be amused by its presumption.

JAMES THURBER: *cartoon caption, New Yorker*
American journalist, writer, and playwright
(1894-1961)

TO THE RED STAINS ON A TABLECLOTH IN A FRENCH RESTAURANT

I look at you with solemn joy wine stain
And push away the plate from where you hide.
My first gulp toasts that unknown man who came
Before me and savored his meal at this table side.

From your lilac edge, spreading like watery hands,
With a drunkard's dreamy tender gaze you peep,
Resembling silhouettes of foreign lands,
Madagascar perhaps or Mozambique.

With golden crumbs my place is now strewn carelessly,
Bread someone slowly broke as he sat down to dine.
O melodic land of fragrant burgundy
Are you the self-same principality
That once a king assessed in tuns of wine?

You, ripe land, played upon by evening light,
Through the mellow tongue of a many-colored prism
Where toll-collectors painted and geniuses took flight,
Where even God forgot his heavenly vision.

I saw you torn with steel and sealed in blood.
In agony I lay on your body, a churned slough.
Perhaps it was he who shot at me from the mud
That friendly, stout sommelier who serves me now.

Ah, didn't I drink at your well of tears that day?
Didn't I see you almost die, suffer your pain?
Sister land! I raise my glass to your rich clay,
At your threshold I kiss every wine and blood stain.

He fills my glass, wine sparkles from the bottle's mouth.
So drink tablecloth, drink like a thirsty dog.
This foreigner bows to your honor, your sunlit south
And heads reluctantly north into the fog.

> CARL ZUCKMAYER
> German dramatist (1896-1977)

There are all sorts of wine, young and old, good and bad, still and sparkling. There are times, moods and occasions when young wine will give us greater pleasure than the old; others when we shall enjoy the company of the old far more than that of the young.

> ALEC WAUGH: *In Praise of Wine*
> English novelist (1898-1981)

I sat in a large airy cafe, listening to sentimental music, sipping a sweet sparkling wine, realizing how wine could not only wash away one's cares but heighten one's big moments.

Wine is one of the most civilized things in the world and one of the natural things of the world that has been brought to the greatest perfection, and it offers a greater range of enjoyment and appreciation than, possibly, any other purely sensory thing which may be purchased.

> ERNEST HEMINGWAY: *Death in the Afternoon*
> American author (1899-1961)

In Europe then we thought of wine as something as healthy and normal as food and also as a great giver of happiness and well being and delight. Drinking wine was not a snobbism nor a sign of sophistication nor a cult; it was as natural as eating and to me as necessary.

> ERNEST HEMINGWAY: *A Moveable Feast*

This wine is too good for toast-drinking, my dear. You don't want to mix emotions up with a wine like that. You lose the taste.

> ERNEST HEMINGWAY: *The Sun Also Rises*

All I want out of wines is to enjoy them.

> ERNEST HEMINGWAY: *The Sun Also Rises*

I drank a bottle of wine for company. It was a Chateau Margaux. It was pleasant to be drinking slowly and to be tasting the wine and to be drinking alone. A bottle of wine was good company.

> ERNEST HEMINGWAY: *The Sun Also Rises*

A person with increasing knowledge and sensory education may derive infinite enjoyment from wine.

> ERNEST HEMINGWAY

I drink [champagne] when I'm happy and when I'm sad. Sometimes I drink it when I'm alone. When I have company I consider it obligatory. I trifle with it if I'm not hungry and drink it when I am. Otherwise I never touch it—unless I'm thirsty.

LILY BOLLINGER: *La Grande Dame du Champagne*
French vintner (1899-1977)

There must always be wine and fellowship or we are truly lost.

ANN FAIRBAIRN
American writer (c. 1901-72)

As food, wine supplies fluids, calories, minerals, vitamins, proteins, and other dietary elements. As medicine, wine may act as an appetite stimulant, stomachic, tonic, tranquilizer, anesthetic, astringent, antiseptic, vasodilator, diaphoretic, diuretic, and antibacterial agent, in addition to its age-old use as a universal menstruum for active therapeutic agents derived from plants. It should be stated that all foods are medicines, and that many medicines are also foods. Like any food, medicine is beneficial in proper dosage, and harmful when taken in excess.

SALVATORE P. LUCIA, M.D.: *A History of Wine as Therapy*
American physician and writer (1901-84)

For wine has participated universally in the cultural ascent of man, serving as a festive drink at his birth, a solemn drink at his death, a sacred drink in religious ceremonies, and a stimulant of discussion in symposium and intellectual colloquia.

SALVATORE P. LUCIA, M.D.: *A History of Wine as Therapy*

Wine was born, not invented....Like an old friend, it continues to surprise us in new and unexpected ways.

SALVATORE P. LUCIA, M.D.

Wine has been utilized with beneficial effects by nearly all cultural groups for thousands of years, not only as food and medicine, but also because of its value in protecting man against the symptoms of tension and stress.

SALVATORE P. LUCIA, M.D.: *A History of Wine as Therapy*

Alcoholism is rare when wine is customarily used with meals, and especially where it is introduced as a food in family surroundings relatively early in childhood.

SALVATORE P. LUCIA, M.D.: *A History of Wine as Therapy*

There is already clear evidence that specific wines are useful as therapeutic aids in uncomplicated cases of diabetes, in simple anemias, in such digestive disturbances as the malabsorption syndrome, in the initial treatment of alcoholic cirrhosis, in minimizing acidosis in certain kidney conditions, in the treatment of anorexia, in relieving the infirmities and suffering which accompany old age, and in combating many of the diseases in which anxiety and tension are among the underlying factors. And it is now beyond conjecture that wine can play a major role in the prevention of alcoholism.

SALVATORE P. LUCIA, M.D.: *A History of Wine as Therapy*

The prescription of wine, with its imposing record as a therapeutic agent, was almost universal, and reached its highest point in medical history during [the seventeenth, eighteenth, and nineteenth centuries]. Here was an important stimulant of appetite, an effective diuretic, and a reliable sedative; a nutritious and pleasant dietary beverage, usually beneficial or at least relatively harmless in most organic disorders, and capable of producing dramatic recoveries in psychosomatic disturbances.

SALVATORE P. LUCIA, M.D.: *A History of Wine as Therapy*

Wine is the most ancient dietary beverage and the most important medicinal agent in continuous use throughout the history of mankind.

176

Wine remains a simple thing, a marriage of pleasure.
> Andre Tchelistcheff
> American winemaker (b. 1901)

Excellent wine generates enthusiasm. And whatever you do with enthusiasm is generally successful.
> Phillippe de Rothschild
> French vintner (1902-1988)

Wine is a bride who brings a great dowry to the man who woos her persistently and gracefully; she turns her back on a rough approach.
> Evelyn Waugh: *Wine in Peace and War*
> English author (1903-66)

[Wine is] exaltation for the mystic; a sense of unity with the whole and of belonging for the disinherited; courage for the timid; peace for the troubled spirit; nepenthe for the tortured soul; aphrodisiac for the lover; surcease for the pain-wracked; anaesthetic for use in surgery; gaiety for the depressed. In addition to its mystical or personal appeal, wine offered pecuniary advantages: vines produce a crop with an ever-ready market. They produce a crop of relatively high value on a wide variety of surfaces and soils: on slopes so steep that almost no other crop can be cultivated and on virtually sterile rocks; thence through a gamut of soils to alluvium; and in a wide variety of climates. They do not demand irrigation. They yield a product that has international appeal and international markets (even in early times). The beverage produced is not only attractive but also healthy in lands of little and often polluted water. It is a persuasive beverage that makes lasting friendships. Once it is known, a permanent and probably increasing market is virtually guaranteed.

DAN STANISLAWSKI: *Dionysus Westward*
American professor, historian, and geographer (b. 1903)

If food is the body of good living, wine is its soul.

CLIFTON FADIMAN
American writer and critic (b. 1904)

The drinking of wine seems to have a moral edge over many pleasures and hobbies in that it promotes love of one's neighbor. As a general thing it is not a lone occupation. A bottle of wine begs to be shared; I have never met a miserly wine lover.

CLIFTON FADIMAN: *The Joys of Wine*

[T]he pleasures of wine, being both sensory and intellectual, are profound. There are few pleasures of which this can be said.

CLIFTON FADIMAN: *The Joys of Wine*

To taste port is to taste a tiny atom of England and her past.

CLIFTON FADIMAN: *The Joys of Wine*

That wine connects with religion, history, legend, myth, literature, and the arts, with space and time—all this is true, and all constitutes part of the joys of wine. But one need not be interested in any of these linkages to love and enjoy wine. For most of us its satisfactions lie squarely (or roundly) within the bottle itself. But what rests in that bottle represents a broad range of possible sensations. It is the unique diversity of wine that is one of its principal charms.

CLIFTON FADIMAN: *The Joys of Wine*

[W]ine is alive, and when you offer it to your fellow man you are offering him life. More than that, you are calling out more life in him, you are engaging in what might be called a creative flattery, for you are asking him to summon up his powers of discrimination, to exercise his taste, or perhaps merely to evince curiosity or a desire to learn. I know no other liquid that, placed in the mouth, forces one to think.

CLIFTON FADIMAN: *The Joys of Wine*

To take wine into our mouths is to savor a droplet of the river of human history.

CLIFTON FADIMAN

A truly great wine with brilliant color, subtle bouquet, perfect balance, and lingering taste is a sensuous experience and a work of art.

KENNETH MACDONALD AND TOM THROCKMORTON:
Drink Thy Wine with a Merry Heart
American authors (b. 1905) and (b. 1913)

[Wine] complements food, it enhances conversation, it adds color and sparkle to the table, and it provides a warm feeling of well-being.

KENNETH MACDONALD AND TOM THROCKMORTON:
Drink Thy Wine with a Merry Heart

To a lover of chardonnay wines, the grape variety announces itself as unmistakably as the theme of Beethoven's Fifth Symphony. No other white grape has a more complex aroma. No other white wine has a more welcome caress as it lingers on the palate.

ELEANOR MCCREA: *University of California Sotheby Book of California Wine*
American vintner (b. 1907)

WOMANOEUVRE

In a carefully thought-out manoeuvre,

My wife sometimes throws down the Hoover,
And insists that we dine
On salmon, with wine
From the Mosel,
the Saar or
the Ruwer. . . .

> CYRIL RAY: *Lickerish Limericks*
> English wine writer (b. 1908)

. . . As the Sparks Fly Upwards

I've tried, but it's always in vain,
Not to drink so much champagne,
But when I'm in trouble
I do need that bubble
—and it happens again and again. . . .

> CYRIL RAY: *Lickerish Limericks*

Wine, that most versatile of drinks, can be enjoyed any-where and at any time. By itself, with a meal, at a celebration or party, its appealing sight, smell, and taste are always welcome.

> CYRIL RAY: *The Guide to Wine*

I can no more think of my own life without thinking of wine and wines and where they grew for me and why I drank them when I did and why I picked the grapes and where I opened the oldest procurable bottles, and all that, than I can remember living before I breathed. In other words, wine is life, and my life and wine are inextricable. And the saving grace of all wine's many graces, probably, is that it can never be dull. It is only the people who try to sing about it who may sound flat. But wine is an older thing than we are, and is forgiving of even the most boring explanation of its *elan vital*.

M. F. K. FISHER: *University of California Sotheby Book of CaliforniaWine*
American writer (b. 1908)

THE HALF FULL GLASS

I told you I was drained of happiness.
The wine was only half-way down our glasses.
You said to me, "Are you not happy now?"
Searching my heart, I had to own I was.
How should I not be, drinking wine with you?
"Whatever dies was not mixed equally,"
Donne said. If so, love is without death,
For half the happiness of meeting you
Is pain at knowing we must separate;
And therefore love can never be complete.
A glass untasted and an empty glass,
Are nothing but mere hope and memory.
The glass in which I drink your health contains
Now and always half wine, half emptiness.

JAMES REEVES
English author (b. 1909)

Wine, it's in my veins and I can't get it out.

BURGESS MEREDITH
American actor and oenophile (b. 1909)

TO THEA AT THE YEAR'S END—
WITH A BOTTLE OF GEWURZTRAMINER

I have no fancy to define
    Love's fullness by what went before;
I think the day we crossed the line
Was when we drank the sea-cooled wine
    Upon a sun-warmed shore.
The sun in sudden strength that day
    Inflamed the air but could not reach

The steel-sharp sea of middle May
That brimmed with cold the breathless bay
   Below the sun-drowned beach.

The sun's heat lay its heavy hand
   On unaccustomed skins as we
Went tip-toe down the tilted strand
And set our bottle on the sand
   To cool it in the sea:

And watched as, where the sea-surge spent
   The last of its quiescent strength,
Stone-cold and circumambient,
The intermittent water went
   Along its polished length.

The bottle took the water's cold
   But did not let its wetness pass;
Glinting and green the water rolled
Against the wine's unmoving gold
   Behind its walls of glass.

We cooled it to our just conceit
   And drank. The cold aroma came
Almost intolerably sweet
To palates which the salt and heat
   Had flayed as with a flame.

We swam and sunned as well as drank,
   And found all heaven in a word;
But, dearest Thea, to be frank,
I think we had the wine to thank
   For most of what occurred.

And now the winter is to waste,
   I bring a bottle like the first;
And this in turn can be replaced,
As long as we have tongues to taste,
   And God shall give us thirst,

Lest with the year our love decline,
   Or like the summer lose its fire,

Before the sun resurgent shine
To warm the sea that cooled the wine
  That kindled our desire.
        P. M. HUBBARD
        American author (b. 1910)

May your every glass of wine be better than the one you had before.

        BROTHER TIMOTHY: *Drink Thy Wine with a Merry Heart*
        American priest and winemaker (b. 1910)

Quality in wines is much easier to recognize than to define.
        MAYNARD A. AMERINE
        Professor Emeritus, Oenology, U.C. Davis (b. 1911)

Winetasting, in the classic phrase, is a diverting pastime for young and old, for ladies as well as men. It is not so intellectual as chamber-music, it is not so light-hearted as striptease; no one will burst into "Ach, du lieber Augustin" as he waves his tiny libation of some promising new vintage around his head, nor will anyone entangle you with problems that need an intimate understanding of Einstein and a slide-rule to answer. It is, in fact, the ideal pursuit with which to while away those hours between eleven in the morning and four in the afternoon.

        B. A. YOUNG
        English writer (b. 1912)

There is no substitute for pulling corks.
        ALEXIS LICHINE
        American author and wine critic (b. 1913)

Wine is the only natural beverage that feeds not only the body, but the soul and spirit of man; stimulates the mind and creates a more gracious and happy way of life.

ROBERT MONDAVI: *Pictorial Atlas to North American Wines*
American winemaker (b. 1913)

Making good wine is a skill, fine wine an art.

ROBERT MONDAVI: *Soul of the Vine*

Wine has been part of the human experience since civilization began. It is the natural beverage for every celebration: births, graduations, engagements, weddings, anniversaries, promotions, family gatherings, meetings with friends, and toasts between governments.

ROBERT MONDAVI: *Beyond the Grapes*

Wine is the temperate, civilized, sacred, romantic mealtime beverage recommended in the Bible. It is a liquid food that has been part of civilization for 8000 years. Wine has been praised for centuries by statesmen, scholars, poets, and philosophers. It has been used as a religious sacrament, as the primary beverage of choice for food, and as a source of pleasure and diversion.

ROBERT MONDAVI: *Plain Talk About Fine Wine*

To make outstanding wines a vintner should maintain a balance between the introduction of modern equipment and the need to maintain the human element. Old timers believe the quality of a man's wine depends on his own quality and character, a little bit of himself going into every bottle. To gain lasting fame he has to be a poet, a philosopher and an honorable man as well as a master craftsman.

PETER MONDAVI
American winemaker (b. 1914)

One cannot imagine the wine drinker in solitude.... The real lover of wine can only enjoy it along with friends, sharing with them the

184

art of conversation and the art of drinking. Wine is indeed essentially a sign of civilization, a factor of sociability, friendship.

JEAN DRAPEAU
Former Mayor of Montreal (b. 1916)

A bunch of grapes is beautiful, static, and innocent. It is merely fruit. But when it is crushed it becomes an animal, for the crushed grapes become wine and wine has an animal life.

WILLIAM YOUNGER: *Gods, Men, and Wine*
(1917-61)

No, Agnes, a Bordeaux is not a house of ill-repute.

GEORGE BAIN: *Champagne is for Breakfast*
Canadian author (b. 1920)

I am neither negative nor defensive about my hobby, really. I suppose, to be brief about it, I could say simply that I like the look, smell, and taste of wine; I like the sorts of places in which it grows; I like the fact that it is a natural product of infinite variety; I like its having a long history; and I like the idea that some time, preferably a long time hence, I will uncork a bottle which will come up to some undefined standard of perfection, whereupon I will exclaim, "That's it"—and quietly and blissfully depart for that Great Wine Cellar in the Sky.

GEORGE BAIN: *Champagne is for Breakfast*

I like [champagne] because it always tastes as though my foot is asleep.

ART BUCHWALD
American writer and journalist (b. 1925)

The important thing with the 1874 Lafite is to taste the wine in its historical context. In 1874 the Impressionists were painting, Brahms was composing and Paris was just over the Commune.

MICHAEL BROADBENT
English wine auctioneer and writer (b. 1927)

VINEYARD FEVER

I must look over the vines again, see the noble vine in the earth.
And all I ask is a strong horse and a saddle round her girth,
And the rein's tug and the nag's smell and the green leaves
    swaying
In a soft breeze from the South West and the old mare neighing.

I must look over the vines again, see the rows and the stony
    soil
And the Merlot with her black grapes and memories of toil;
And all I ask is a cloudless sky with the bright sun burning
And ten more days and nine more nights with no rain
    returning.

I must look over the vines again where my childhood days
    were spent,
See the young roots and the old roots which have now become
    gnarled and bent;
And all I ask is a jug of wine from the grapes my sons have
    tended,
And to know the vineyard will yet be tilled when the long
    day's ended.

ROBIN BLACKBURNE
English wine merchant, writer, and Master of Wine
(b. 1933)

Wine is like music—you may not know what is good, but
you know what you like!

JUSTIN MEYER: *Plain Talk About Fine Wine*
American winemaker (b. 1938)

I recently had the pleasure of lunching with a very classy lady. I'd
have to call her elderly because she must have been close to 70, yet
she had that twinkle in her eyes that told you she would never grow
old. Someone brought up the quote… [A meal without wine is like

a day without sunshine.] and her reply was, "A meal without wine is like making love by yourself."

JUSTIN MEYER: *Plain Talk About Fine Wine*

Wine is food; it should taste good. It should be fun; you should look forward to it and not be intimidated by it. While there may be lousy wine, there's no such thing as the wrong wine. Maybe you just served it to the wrong people. Maybe you just read the wrong reviewer. So get out there and experiment. Let your palate be your guide and for goodness sakes—enjoy yourself!

JUSTIN MEYER: *Plain Talk About Fine Wine*

Wine has certain properties that mattered much more to our ancestors than to ourselves. For 2000 years of medical and surgical history it was the universal and unique antiseptic. Wounds were bathed with it; water made safe to drink.

HUGH JOHNSON: *The Story of Wine*
English wine writer (b. 1939)

The more I have learned about wine in the course of a quarter of a century of enjoyment, the more I have realized that it weaves in with human history from its very beginnings as few, if any, other products do. Textiles, pottery, bread. . . there are other objects of daily use that we can also trace back to the Stone Age. Yet wine alone is charged with sacramental meaning, with healing powers; indeed with a life of its own.

Why is wine so special? Partly because for most of its history, and mankind's, it has been his one source of comfort and courage, his only medicine and antiseptic, his one recourse to renew his tired spirits and lift him above his weary, saddened self. Wine was the foremost of luxuries to millenia of mankind.

HUGH JOHNSON: *The Story of Wine*

Wine is the pleasantest subject in the world to discuss. All its associations are with occasions when people are at their best; with relaxation, contentment, leisurely meals and the free flow of ideas. The scope of the subject of wine is never-ending. It is its fascination to me that so many other subjects lie within its boundaries. Without geography and topography it is incomprehensible; without history it is colourless; without taste it is meaningless; without travel it remains unreal. It embraces botany, chemistry, agriculture, carpentry, economics—any number of sciences whose names I do not even know. It leads you up paths of knowledge and byways of expertise you would never glimpse without it. Best of all, it brings you into friendly contact with some of the most skillful and devoted craftsmen, most generous and entertaining hosts you would find anywhere.

HUGH JOHNSON: *Wine*

Wine has the most precious quality that art has: it makes ideas, people, incidents, places, sensations seem larger than life.

HUGH JOHNSON: *Wine*

Wine is like sex in that few men will admit not knowing all about it.

HUGH JOHNSON

If you pay attention to it, a good wine will always have something to tell you. What exactly it says no one can ever completely understand, of course, and that is wine's charm and its mystery.

JAMES NORWOOD PRATT: *The Wine Bibber's Bible*
American wine writer (b. 1942)

Good wine is nothing to rave about, but it is something to be thankful for. Fine wine, on the other hand, is a blessing.

JAMES NORWOOD PRATT: *The Wine Bibber's Bible*

As in lovemaking, reading is a damn poor substitute for experience in the gentle art of [wine] tasting. It is one of those things you find out for by yourself.

JAMES NORWOOD PRATT: *The Wine Bibber's Bible*

Light the candles and pour the red wine into your glass. Before you begin to eat, raise your glass in honor of yourself. The company is the best you'll ever have.

> DANIEL HALPERN
> American poet (b. 1945)

Champagne is the wine-lover's luxury.

> JANCIS ROBINSON: *The Great Wine Book*
> English wine writer and Master of Wine (b. 1950)

Great wine inspires, impresses, invigorates, and, perhaps most significantly of all, intrigues.

> JANCIS ROBINSON: *The Great Wine Book*

Sometimes you have to stop and sniff the corks.

> ARNA DAN ISACSSON
> Swedish oenophile (b. 1962)

Warm Dom is better than cold Bud.

> ANGELA F. BUNGER
> American oenophile (b. 1964)

Beer is the bread of alcohol,
Wine is the entertainment.

> LANA ELTON
> American oenophile (b. 1970)

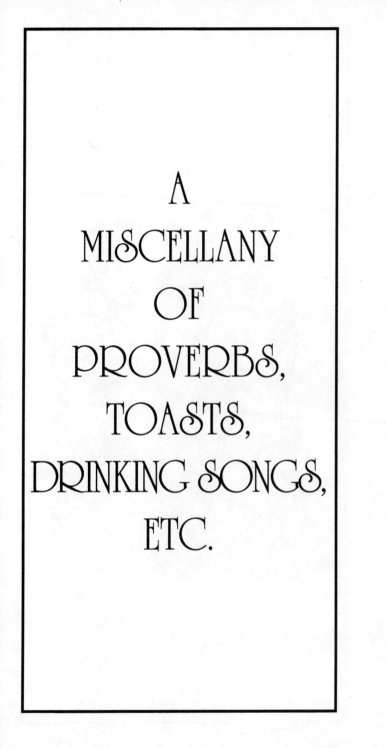

A
MISCELLANY
OF
PROVERBS,
TOASTS,
DRINKING SONGS,
ETC.

It is difficult to say where the custom of "toasting" originated because much of this common practice is based in legend. We do know, however, that it existed during ancient civilizations of the Greeks, Romans, and Saxons, and has continued to be a part of most cultures throughout history.

One theory of origin suggests that during the days of the ancient empires, when many of the various factions were continually warring with one another, toasting came about during the peace agreements. The ruler of the conquering or hosting empire would stand and take the first drink of wine to assure his former enemies that the beverage was not poisoned and that he could, therefore, be trusted as an honorable person. Toasting then evolved so that it was included at other ceremonial occasions, as well.

A popular mythological legend explaining the custom of raising glasses in a toast identifies Dionysus, the god of wine, as the originator. He supposedly included the practice of clinking glasses in a toast so that all of the human senses could thereby be stimulated whenever his sacred beverage of wine was consumed. Wine already affected the senses of taste, sight, touch, and smell—only hearing was left out, so Dionysus rectified the problem by initiating the toast.

Actually, toasting was not called "toasting" until the sixteenth century when the custom of adding toasted bread to wine became fashionable in England. After reciting a "toast," the bread was removed from the wine and consumed; thus, people began calling for "toasts" to honor specific occasions or people.

Toasting became an art form as the toasters tried to outdo each other with their recitations. Poetry, proverbs, limericks, and drinking songs all were included when glasses were raised in celebration. Some of these toasts have been part of cultural traditions for centuries, and while there are toasts to honor practically everyone and everything, the ones assembled here specifically honor wine.

One barrel of wine can work more miracles than a church full of saints.

ITALIAN PROVERB

In water one sees one's own face; but in wine one beholds the heart of another.

FRENCH PROVERB

Wine softens a hard bed.

SPANISH PROVERB

All wine would be port if it could.

PORTUGUESE PROVERB

Rhine wine, fine wine.

GERMAN PROVERB

When the time to drink wine comes, drink it.

CHINESE PROVERB

With spicy food drink plenty of wine.

SPANISH PROVERB

It is only the first bottle of wine that is expensive.

FRENCH PROVERB

If the sea were wine, everyone would be a sailor.

SPANISH PROVERB

Wine is a discoverer of secrets.

CHINESE PROVERB

Brandy is lead in the morning, silver at noon, and gold at night.

GERMAN PROVERB

As long as we have wine, a pack of cards, and a fire, let anything happen.

SPANISH PROVERB

Good wine needs no crier.

FRENCH PROVERB

Half a cup of wine brings tears, a full cup laughter.

KOREAN PROVERB

He who has wealth and wine will always have friends.

CHINESE PROVERB

The best use of bad wine is to drive away poor relations.

FRENCH PROVERB

For wine to taste like wine, it should be drunk with a friend.

SPANISH PROVERB

Of a brave man and a good wine, ask not whence they came.

GERMAN PROVERB

With a dear friend a thousand cups of wine are too few.

CHINESE PROVERB

Good wine praises itself.

ARAB PROVERB

Drink a glass of wine after your soup, and you steal a ruble from the doctor.

RUSSIAN PROVERB

When the head is under the influence of wine, many a thing swims out of the heart.

YUGOSLAVIAN PROVERB

Wine will not keep in a foul vessel.

FRENCH PROVERB

Over a bottle of wine many a friend is found.

YIDDISH PROVERB

Water for oxen, wine for kings.

SPANISH PROVERB

Wine poured out is not wine swallowed.

FRENCH PROVERB

Three glasses of wine can set everything to rights.

CHINESE PROVERB

Every cask smells of the wine it contains.

SPANISH PROVERB

Wine is the best broom for troubles.

JAPANESE PROVERB

Friends and wine should be old.

SPANISH PROVERB

Wine wears no breeches.
FRENCH PROVERB

There are more old wine drinkers than old doctors.
GERMAN PROVERB

Water for fish, wine for men.
SPANISH PROVERB

White meat, white wine; red meat, red wine.
FRENCH PROVERB

If wine interferes with your business, put your business aside.
SPANISH PROVERB

Burgundy for kings, champagne for duchesses, and claret for gentlemen.
FRENCH PROVERB

No wine, no company; no wine, no conversation.
CHINESE PROVERB

Money spent taking care of good wine is money well spent.
FRENCH PROVERB

Wine on milk is good; milk on wine is poison.
FRENCH PROVERB

After melon, wine is a felon.
ITALIAN PROVERB

Without bread, without wine, love is nothing.
    FRENCH PROVERB

Wine should sparkle, cheese should weep, and bread should sing.
    SPANISH PROVERB

Who buys good wine will taste and drink good wine.
    FRENCH PROVERB

Good wine gladdens the eye, cleans the teeth, and heals the stomach.
    SPANISH PROVERB

Wine does not intoxicate men; men intoxicate themselves.
    CHINESE PROVERB

The human heart rejoices in good wine.
    LATIN PROVERB

For a bad night, a mattress of wine.
    SPANISH PROVERB

Wine is the greatest medicine.
    JEWISH SAYING

Wine helps open the heart to reason.
    JEWISH SAYING

Wine is old men's milk.
    MEDIEVAL LATIN SAYING

Drink wine, and you will sleep well.
Sleep, and you will not sin.
Avoid sin, and you will be saved.
Ergo, drink wine and be saved.

    MEDIEVAL GERMAN SAYING

By the bread and the salt, by the water and wine,
Thou art welcome, friend, at this board of mine.

    FRENCH TOAST

May your love be like good wine, and grow stronger as it
grows older.

    OLD ENGLISH TOAST

Baths, wine, and Venus bring decay to our bodies,
But baths, wine, and Venus make life worth living.

    LATIN EPITAPH

Back of this wine is the vintner,
And back through the years his skill,
And back of it all are the vines in the sun
And the rain and the Master's Will.

    VINTNER'S ODE

Wine pours into our mouths; you can smell it, feel it and
drink it. I prefer it to music, flowers or the heavens.

    FRENCH FOLK SONG

Let us praise God with this symbol of joy and thank Him for
the blessings of the past week, for life and strength, for home
and love and friendship, for the discipline of our trials and
temptations, for the happiness that has come to us out of our
labors. . . . Praised be thou, O Lord our God, King of the
universe, who hast created the fruit of the vine.

    JEWISH PRAYER

Wine the good and bland, thou blessing
Of the good, the bad's distressing,
Sweet of taste by all confessing,
 Hail, thou world's felicity!
Hail thy hue, life's gloom dispelling
Hail thy taste, all tastes expelling;
By thy power, in this thy dwelling
 Deign to make us drunk with thee!

Oh, how blest for bounteous uses
Is the birth of pure wine-juices!
Safe's the table which produces
 Wine in goodly quality.
Oh, in color how auspicious!
Oh, in odour how delicious!
In the mouth how sweet, propitious
 To the tongue enthralled by thee.

Blest the man who first thee planted,
Called thee by thy name enchanted!
He whose cups have ne'er been scanted
 Dreads no danger that may be.
Blest the belly where thou bidest!
Blest the tongue where thou residest!
Blest the mouth through which thou glidest,
 And the lips thrice blessed by thee!

Therefore let wine's praise be sounded,
Healths to topers all propounded;
We shall never be confounded,
 Toping for eternity!
Pray we: here be thou still flowing,
Plenty on our board bestowing,
While with jocund voice we're showing
 How we serve thee—Jubilee!
  LATIN SONG

The art of tasting wine is the performance of a sacred rite, which deserves to be carried out with the most grave and serious attention.

  FRENCH NATIONAL COMMITTEE FOR WINE PUBLICITY

Let misers in garrets lay up their gay store
And keep their rich bags to live wretchedly poor;
'Tis the cellar alone with true fame is renowned,
Her treasure's diffusive, and cheers all around.
The gold and the gems but the eyes' gaudy toy,
But the Vintner's red juice gives health, love and joy.

SONG OF THE VINTNER'S COMPANY

Come, friends, let us drink again,
This liquid from the nectar vine,
For water makes you dumb and stupid,
Learn this from the fishes—
They cannot sing, nor laugh, nor drink
This beaker full of sparkling wine.

OLD DUTCH SONG

O blessed art thou, O Lord God of our fathers, King of the
Universe, who bringeth forth the fruit of the vine; blessed art
thou, O Lord God of our fathers, King of the Universe, who
bringeth forth bread from the earth; blessed art thou, O Lord
God of our fathers, King of the Universe, who putteth compassion into the hearts of men.

OLD TABLE GRACE

To Burgundy

Hail, Burgundy, thou juice divine,
    Inspirer of my song:—
The praises given to other wine
    To thee alone belong.
Of poignant wit and rosy charms,
    Thou can'st the power improve,
Care of its sting thy balm disarms,
    Thou noblest gift of Jove!

INSCRIBED TO THE MUSICAL SOCIETY, AT THE FIVE
BELLS TAVERN IN THE STRAND

In a Jerez Bodega

Here is wine all dedicated
To the use of Kings and Lords,
Noble casks, ne'er emulated,
Choicest vintage Spain affords.
Decked with names of highest splendour,
Dight with arms of brightest hue,
Princes have been proud to render
Here, to Xeres, homage due.

From the stately courts of hist'ry
Monarchs journeyed to behold
All the ancient art and myst'ry
Of the wood that shrines the gold;
Of the sun, now captivated
In the softly-sleeping wine,
Of our Mother Earth created
To bring forth the fruitful vine.

Here they found the richest treasure
E'en a sovereign can command,
Kings' consoler, Princes' pleasure,
Wisdom's found in ev'ry land.
Worthy wine for royal favour,
Source of peace and all goodwill,
Chivalry knows nothing braver
Than the duty these fulfil.

Here are casks all dedicated,
Wine of rarest pedigree,
Never to be contemplated
Till a king shall bring a key.
What though some make no returning,
Thrones now dust and homage cold?
Here their fame's still brightly burning
In the wood that shrines the gold.

FROM THE VISITORS' BOOK AT GONZALEZ BYASS' JEREZ
BODEGA

Oɴ ᴀ Cʜʀɪsᴛᴍᴀs Pʀᴇsᴇɴᴛ

My grateful glass is lifted to the fine
Scholar who, when he found a precious wine,
Conveyed his sense of the supremely good,
Bringing it where it could be understood.
Having the best that Burgundy could send,
He gave it to no ordinary friend:
For one whose bounty spreads like gracious air,
The scholar found pure joy, a joy to share,
And, to make sure 'twas all that he could think it,
Companionably came and helped to drink it.
Long may such academic courtesies
Flourish; no fear that they should cease to please:
The scholar's gift to all that Christmas lent
A bouquet of the Chambertin he sent.

Pʀᴏᴠᴏsᴛ ᴏғ Tʀɪɴɪᴛʏ Cᴏʟʟᴇɢᴇ: ᴛᴏ ᴏɴᴇ ᴏғ ʜɪs ᴘʀᴏғᴇssᴏʀs

Bᴀᴄᴄʜᴜs, Gᴏᴅ ᴏғ Rᴏsʏ Wɪɴᴇ

Bacchus, god of rosy wine,
Shed your influence divine;
Fill to the brim the sprightly bowl,
Nought but wine can cheer the soul.

By this Alexander fought;
By this godlike Plato thought:
This was, sure, the sacred spring
Where the muses used to sing.

Mirth by this will ever smile,
This will ev'ry care beguile;
Ev'ry joy and social bliss
Rises hence and moves to this.

Love may beat his soft alarms,
This excels e'en Nancy's charms;
Often frowns deform her face,
Wine has everlasting grace.

DRINKING SONG

A Friend and Good Wine

Sum up all the delights this world doth produce,
The darling allurements now chiefly in use,
You'll find, if compared, there's none can contend
With the solid enjoyments of bottle and friend.

For honour, and wealth, and beauty may waste,
These joys often fade, and rarely do last,
They're so hard to attain, and so easily lost,
That the pleasure ne'er answers the trouble and cost.

None but wine and true friendship are lasting and sure,
From jealousy free, and from envy secure;
Then fill all the glasses until they run o'er,
A friend and good wine are the charms we adore.

DRINKING SONG

The Jovial Drinker

A plague on those fools who proclaim against wine,
And fly the dear sweets that the bottle doth bring;
It heightens the fancy, the wit does refine,
And he that was first drunk was made the first king.

By the help of good claret old age becomes youth,
And sick men still find this the only physician;
Drink largely, you'll know by experience the truth,
That he that drinks most is the best politician.

To victory this leads on the brave cavalier,
And makes all the terrors of war but delight;
This flushes his courage, and beats off base fear,
'Twas that that taught Caesar and Pompey to fight.

This supports all our friends, and knocks down all our foes,
This makes all men loyal from courtier to clown.
Like Dutchman from brandy, from this our strength grows;
So 'tis wine, noble wine, that's a friend to the crown.

On a Pint of Sack

Old poets Hippocrene admire,
And pray to water to inspire
Their wit and Muse with heav'nly fire;
Had they this heav'nly fountain seen,
Sack both their well and Muse had been,
And this pint-pot their Hippocrene.

Had they truly discovered it,
They had, like me, thought it unfit
To pray to water for their wit;
And had adored sack as divine,
And made a poet-god of wine,
And this pint-pot had been a shrine.

Sack unto them had been instead
Of nectar, and their heav'nly bread,
And ev'ry boy a Ganymede;
Or had they made a god of it,
Or styled it patron of their wit,
This pot had been a temple fit.

Well then, companions, is't not fit,
Since to this gem we owe our wit,
That we should praise the cabinet,
And drink a health to this divine
And bounteous palace of our vine?
Die he with thirst that doth repine.

Noah to His Sons

Take this, he said, and held aloft
A vine stock branching fair.
Heaven's noblest gift to human kind
Entrusted to thy care.
Go plant it on the sunny hills,
For health and length of days,
And press its fruit for joyous drinks
And the creator's praise.

To Tokay

Blessed be the vines whose amber life,
Gave us Tokay.
Those vineyards, may they thrive,
And send more wine to us,
Of like bouquet.

Praise of the Vine

There is no tre that growe
On earthe, that I do knowe,
More worthie praise, I trowe,
  Than is the vyne;
Whose grapes, as ye may reade,
Theire licoure forthe dothe shede,
Wherof is made indede
  All our good wyne.
And wyne, ye may trust me,
Causeth men for to be
Merie, for so ye se
  His nature is.

Quaff with Me the Purple Wine

Quaff, quaff with me the purple wine,
With me in social pleasures join,
Crown, crown with me thy flowing hair,
Love, love with me the beauteous fair,
And dance off heavy, heavy care.

Wine inspires the patriot soul,
Makes the rigid fair one sigh,
Freedom lies within the bowl,
Love and Friendship, social tie—
Then let's laugh, be gay and free.

THE JOLLY BACCHANAL

Come, all ye jolly Bacchanals,
That love to tope good wine,
Let's offer up a hogshead
Unto our Master's shrine,
Then let us drink and never shrink,
For I'll tell you the reason why:
'Tis a great sin to leave a house
'Till we've drained the cellar dry.

In times of old I was a fool,
I drank the water clear,
But Bacchus took me from that rule;
He thought 'twas too severe.
He fill'd a goblet to the brim,
And he bade me take a sup,
And had it been a gallon pot,
By Jove I'd tossed it up.

And ever since that happy time,
Good wine has been my cheer.
Now nothing puts me in a swoon,
But water or small beer;
Then let us tope about, my boys,
And never flinch nor fly,
But fill our skins brimful of wine,
And drain the bottles dry.

Wine is the liquor of life,
The heart is consumed by care,
Good fellows, then, end the strife
'Twixt the bottle and despair.

Brisk wine and impertinent Care
Dispute the control of me;
Let me be thy master Care,
Wine, thou shalt thy mistress be.

DRINKING SONG

A Pleasant Pint of Poetical Sherry

Come hither, learned Sisters,
    And leave your forked mountain,
I will tell you where is a well
    Doth far exceed your fountain,
Of which, if any poet
    Do taste in some good measure,
It straight doth fill up his head and quill
    With ditties full of pleasure;
And makes him sing, give me sack, old sack, boys,
    To make the Muses merry,
The life of mirth, and the joy of the earth
    Is a cup of good old sherry!

It is the true Nepenthes
    Which makes a sad man frolic,
And doth redress all heaviness,
    Cold agues and the colic;
It takes away the crutches
    From men are lame and crippled,
And dries the pose, and rheums of the nose,
    If it be soundly tippled.
Then let us drink old sack, old sack, boys,
    Which makes us sound and merry,
The life of mirth, and the joy of the earth,
    Is a cup of good old sherry!

It is the river Lethe
    Where men forget their crosses,
And by this drink they never think
    Of poverty and losses;
It gives a man fresh courage,
    If well he sup this nectar,
And cowards soft it lifts aloft,
    And makes them stout as Hector:
Then let us drink old sack, old sack, boys,
    Which makes us stout and merry,
The life of mirth, and the joy of the earth,
    Is a cup of good old sherry!

It is the well of concord,
  Where men do take up quarrels,
When love doth lack, by drinking sack,
  They draw it in from the barrels;
If drunkards are unruly,
  Whom claret hath inflamed,
With a cup or two, this sack can do,
  They sleep, and so are tamed.
Then let us drink old sack, old sack, boys,
  Which makes us kind and merry,
The life of mirth, and the joy of the earth,
  Is a cup of good old sherry!

The knot of hearty friendship
  Is by good sack combined,
They love no jars, nor mortal wars,
  That are to sack inclined;
Nor can he be dishonest,
  Whom sack and sugar feedeth,
For all men see, he's fat and free,
  And no ill humour breedeth:
Then let us drink old sack, old sack, boys,
  That makes us fat and merry,
The life of mirth, and the joy of the earth,
  Is a cup of good old sherry!

[Wine] sloweth age, it strengtheneth youth, it helpeth digestion, it abandoneth melancholie, it relisheth the heart, it lighteneth the mind, it quickeneth the spirits, it keepeth and preserveth the head from whirling, the eyes from dazzling, the tongue from lisping, the mouth from snaffling, the teeth from chattering, and the throat from rattling; it keepeth the stomach from wambling, the heart from swelling, the hands from shivering, the sinews from shrinking, the veins from crumbling, the bones from aching, and the marrow from soaking.

13TH CENTURY ANONYMOUS

Drink! Drink! The Red, Red Wine

Drink! drink! the red, red wine,
That in the goblet glows,
Is hallow'd by the blood that stain'd
The ground whereon it grows.

Drink! drink! there's health and joy
In its foam to the free and brave;
But 'twould blister up like the elf-king's cup
The pale lip of the slave!

Drink! drink! and as your hearts
Are warm'd by its ruddy tide,
Swear to live as free as your fathers liv'd,
Or to die as your fathers died.

To Champagne

Nectar strained to finest gold,
Sweet as Love,
As virtue cold.

Whoever it was
Who distilled this wine
Must have distilled it
Turning his drum
On one side for a mortar,
While singing songs;
He must have distilled it
While dancing.
That must be why this wine,
This wine
Is so extraordinarily enjoyable.
     Sa sa!

        Japanese drinking song (c. 213 A.D.)

210

This wine
    Is not my wine;
It is the wine which
The ruler of wine,
    He who dwells in the Eternal World,
The rock-standing
    God Sukuna,
Divinely blessed,
    Blessed with fury,
Abundantly blessed,
    Blessed going around,
And presented.
Drink deeply.
    Sa sa!
                    JAPANESE DRINKING SONG (C. 213 A.D.)

I have become drunk
On the wine distilled
By Susukori;
I have become drunk
On this wine of peace,
This wine of laughter.
                    JAPANESE DRINKING SONG (4TH CENTURY A.D.)

Love and wine are the bonds that fasten us all,
The world but for these to confusion would fall,
Were it not for the pleasures of love and good wine,
Mankind, for each trifle their lives would resign;
They'd not value dull life nor could live without thinking,
Nor would kings rule the world but for love and good
drinking.
                    TOAST OF 1675

The best glass of white wine is the first,
The best glass of red is the last.

Here's to the magic of bubbling wine
An evening with friends so true
There's none I'd rather enjoy them with
Than you, and you, and you.

May the brimming bowl with a wreath be crowned,
    And quaff the draught divine!
Comrades, not in the world is found
    Such another wine.

How sweet to mark the pouting vine,
Ready to fall in tears of wine;
Where the embowering branches meet—
Oh! is not this divinely sweet?

Then here's to thee, old friend; and long
    May thou and I thus meet,
To brighten still with wine and song
    The short life ere it fleet.

Come, fill a bumper, fill it round,
May mirth, wine and wit abound;
In them alone true wisdom lies—
For to be merry's to be wise.

Let wine, gay comrades, be the food we're fed upon;—
Our amber cheeks its ruby light to shed upon!
Wash us in't, when we die; and let the trees
Of our vineyards yield the bier that we lie dead upon!

For of all labours, none transcend
The works that on the brain depend;
Nor could we finish great designs
Without the power of generous wines.

Good wine is not necessarily dear wine.

Wine is good,
Love is good,
And all is good if understood;
The sin is not in doing,
But in overdoing.
How much of mine has gone that way!
Alas! how much more that may!

By wine we are generous made,
It furnishes fancy with wings;
Without it we ne'er should have had
Philosophers, poets, or kings.

The aperitif, Dry Vermouth—
A zestful wine, and very couth.

If any mortal rash should dare
To cast a slur on wine divine,
Toss him in the depths of ocean
And let him pickle in the brine!
While we enjoy our holidays,
And drink and sing our jolly lays!

May our wine brighten the rays of friendship, but never
diminish its lustre.

Pour deep the rosy wine and drink a toast with me:
Here's to the three:--Thee, Wine, and Camaraderie!

May our wine brighten the mind and strengthen the
resolution.

Had Neptune, when he first took charge of the sea,
Been as wise or at least been as merry as we,
He'd have thought better on't and instead of his brine
Would have filled up the vast ocean with generous wine.

Come goblet—nymph, of heavenly shape,
Pour the rich weepings of the grape.
Song and Wine and Bacchic mirth
Are the best of things on earth.
Wisely, then, it seemeth me,
Men engage in revelry.

While I look in Pleasure's eye
All my powers multiply.
When I drink, the bliss is mine;
There's bliss in every drop of wine!

When wine enlivens the heart
May friendship surround the table.

Come, fill up your glasses, and join in the chant,
For no pleasure's like drinking good wine, you must grant;
Then let this be our toast, may we never repine,
May we ne'er want a friend, or a glass of wine.

The generous wine brings joy divine,
     And beauty charms our soul;
I, while on earth, will still with mirth
     Drink—beauty and the bowl.

Wine, wit, and wisdom.
Wine enough to sharpen wit,
Wit enough to give zest to wine,
Wisdom enough to "shut down" at the right time.

May the juice of the grape enliven each soul,
And good humour preside at the head of each bowl.

Rain makes the vines grow,
the vines make the wine flow,
Oh, Lord! Let it Rain!

May our wine add wings to old time, but not make us
insensible to his flight.

Fill to him, to the brim!
    Round the table let it roll.
The divine says that wine
    Cheers the body and the soul.

The miser may be pleased with gold,
    The sporting man with pretty lass;
But I'm best pleased when I behold
    The nectar sparkling in the glass.

Here's to our next joyous meeting--and, oh, when we meet,
May our wine be as bright and our union as sweet.

But as thy meat, so thy immortal wine
    Makes the smirk face of each to shine,
And spring fresh rosebuds, while the salt, the wit,
    Flows from the wine, and graces it.

Gods my life, what glorious claret!
Blessed be the ground that bore it!
'Tis Avignon. Don't say a flask of it;
Into my soul I pour a cask of it.

O, Bacchus who hath sent us wine,
Give us now, we pray,
Wit with drink.

May all the sweets of life combine,
Mirth and music, love and wine.
For I know that Death is a guest divine,
Who shall drink my blood as I drink this wine;
And he cares for nothing—a king is he!
Come on, old fellow, and drink with me!
With you I will drink to the solemn past,
Though the cup that I drain should be my last.

Would you be a man in fashion?
    Would you lead a life divine?
Take a little Dram of Passion
    In a lusty dose of wine.

May friendship, like wine, improve as time advances,
And may we always have old wine, old friends, and young
cares.

Here's to this water,
    Wishing it were wine,
Here's to you, my darling,
    Wishing you were mine.

May your generous heart, like good wine,
Only grow mellower with the years.

The diamond sleeps within the mine,
    The pearl beneath the water;
While Truth, more precious, dwells in wine,
    The grape's own rosy daughter.

Here's to the triple alliance—Friendship, Freedom, and Wine.

The goblets fill to brimming,
     Hail the vintage rich and glowing,
In the goblets redly flowing,
Like a baby Cupid's crowing;
     This our festival will grace!
Hail the Wine that wakens laughter
From the cellar to the rafter,
Leaving care to follow after—
     Leading him a pretty chase!

Before our fading years decline,
Let us quaff the brimming wine.

Come, fill the glass and drain the bowl;
     May Love and Bacchus still agree;
And every American warm his soul
     With Cupid, Wine, and Liberty.

O little fishes of the sea,
     Had I the power divine,
I'd turn ye into silver cups
     And your sea to purple wine.

O grant me, kind Bacchus,
     The god of the vine,
Not a pipe nor a tun,
But an ocean of wine...
So that, living or dead,
     Both body and spirit
May float round the world
In an ocean of claret.

If the nymph have no compassion,
Vain it is to sigh or groan;
Love was but put in for fashion,
Wine will do the work alone.

God made man, frail as a bubble;
Man made love—love made trouble.
God made the vine—
Then is it a sin
That man made wine
To drown trouble in?

Friendship's the wine of life.
Let's drink of it and to it.

Let with a wreath the brimming bowl be crowned,
And quaff the draught divine!
Sir Topers, not in Europe to be found
Is such another wine.

Now, now, my friends, the gathering gloom
With roseate rays of wine illume;
And while our wreaths of parsley spread
Their fadeless foliage round our head,
Let's hymn the almighty power of wine,
And shed libations on his shrine!

Here's to Water, water divine—
It dews the grapes that give us wine.

To the sun that warmed the vineyard,
To the juice that turned to wine,
To the host who cracked the bottle,
And made it yours and mine.

Those blessed lands, those blessed lands,
    Where summer sun never burns,
Where winter winds never chill,
    Where all the earth labors gently,
To produce its fruitfulness,
    Where the grape is sweet,
And its wine nourishes the very soul of man.

Here's to champagne, the drink divine
That makes us forget our troubles;
It's made of a dollar's worth of wine
And three dollars worth of bubbles.

Life is too short to drink bad wine.

Go pluck the grape,
    Lest the sprite escape
That lurks 'neath its purple cover;
    Go rob the vine
    Of the soul of wine,
And sing and dream like a lover.

Nothing can match the joy of the wine-drinker save the joy
of the wine being drunk.

Here's to the wine which held a store
Of imprisoned joy and laughter!
Here's to this bottle, many more bottles,
And to those who follow after.

A warm toast.
Good company.
A fine wine.
May you enjoy all three.

With each glass of this wine, I double the number of friends
I have in this room.

Wine is the whetstone to wit.

There's no sweet in the world to measure
 With the juice of the golden vine;
There's no delicate new-born pleasure
 That can rival the rapture of wine.
Then let's not fear its fragrant perfume—
 Good wine's been defamed too long;
For if it steals away your reason,
 It gives us love, laughter, and song.

Wine improves with age—I like it more the older I get.

To you, and yours, and theirs, and mine,
I pledge with you, their health in wine.

Water separates the people of the world, wine unites them.

God in his goodness sent the grapes
To cheer both great and small;
Little fools will drink too much
And great fools none at all.

Here's to the heart that fills as the wine bottle empties.

May we never want for wine, nor for a friend
o help drink it.

WORKS CONSULTED

Adams, A. K., comp. *The Home Book of Humorous Quotations*. New York: Dodd, 1969.

Alderson, William A., ed. *Here's to You*. New York: Dodge, 1908.

Allen, Herbert Warner. *A Contemplation of Wine*. London: Michael Joseph, 1951.
——. *A History of Wine: Great Vintage Wines from the Homeric Age to the Present Day*. New York: Horizon, 1961.
——. *The Romance of Wine*. New York: Dover, 1932.

Amerine, M. A. and V. L. Singleton. *Wine: An Introduction*. 2d ed. Berkeley: U of California P, 1977.

Anacreon. *The Odes of Anacreon*. Translated by Thomas Moore. New York: G. P. Putnam's Sons, 1903.

Antrium, Minna Thomas, ed. *A Book of Toasts*. Philadelphia: Henry Altemus, 1902.

Aristophanes. *Aristophanes*. Vol 1. Translated by Benjamin Bickley Rogers. Cambridge: Harvard UP, 1924.

Aye, John. *The Humour of Drinking*. London: Universal, 1934.

Bacchylides. *Bacchylides: The Poems and Fragments*. Edited by Richard C. Jebb. Hildesheim: Georg Olms, 1967.

Bain, George. *Champagne is for Breakfast*. Toronto: New Press, 1972.

Bartlett, John, ed. *Bartlett's Familiar Quotations*. 14th ed. Boston: Little, 1968.

Baudelaire, Charles. *The Poems of Charles Baudelaire*. Translated by F. P. Sturm. New York: AMS, 1981.

Benson, Robert, ed. *Great Winemakers of California*. Santa Barbara, CA: Capra, 1977.

Benwell, W. S. *Journey to Wine in Victoria*. Melbourne: Sir Isaac Pitman, 1960.

Berger, Dan and Richard Paul Hinkle. *Beyond the Grapes: An Inside Look at Napa Valley*. Wilmington: Atomium, 1991.

Berry, Charles Walter. *Viniana*. London: Constable, 1934.

Bespaloff, Alexis, ed. *The Fireside Book of Wine: An Anthology for Wine Drinkers*. New York: Simon & Schuster, 1972.

Billings, Henry. *The Joys of Cheap Wine*. Shelburne, VT: New England, 1984.

Blackburne, Robin. *Vintage Versage: A Collection of Rhymes, Parodies, and Wine Nonsense*. Hamilton, Bermuda: Balmoral, 1984.

Blue, Anthony Dias. *American Wine: A Comprehensive Guide*. New York: Doubleday, 1985.

Bohle, Bruce, ed. *The Home Book of American Quotations*. New York: Dodd Mead, 1967.

Bohn, Henry G., ed. *A Polyglot of Foreign Proverbs*. New York: AMS, 1968.

Brillat-Savarin, Anthelme. *Brillat-Savarin's "The Physiology of Taste."* Translated by M. F. K. Fisher. New York: Harcourt Brace Jovanovich, 1949.

Broadbent, Michael. *Complete Guide to Wine Tasting and Wine Cellars*. New York: Simon & Schuster, 1984.

Brooks, Fred Emerson, ed. *Buttered Toasts*. Chicago: Forbes, 1911.

Brussell, Eugene E., ed. *Dictionary of Quotable Definitions*. Englewood Cliffs, NJ: Prentice-Hall, 1970.

Burns, Robert. *The Poetical Works of Robert Burns*. Edited by Rev. Robert Aris Wilmott. London: George Routledge, n.d.

Byron, Lord [George Gordon]. *Lord Byron: Don Juan*. Edited by Leslie A. Marchand. Boston: Houghton Mifflin, 1958.

Carruth, Gorton and Eugene Ehrlich, eds. *American Quotations*. New York: Wings Books, 1988.

Carter, Everett. *Wine and Poetry*. Davis: U of California Library, 1976.

Cato. *Cato the Censor on Farming*. Translated by Ernest Brehaut. New York: Octagon, 1966.

Chase, Edith Lea and W. E. P. French, eds. *Waes Hael: The Book of Toasts*. New York: Grafton, 1904.

Chesterton, G. K. *Wine, Water, and Song*. 20th ed. London: Methuen, 1946.

Clotho, comp. *Prosit: A Book of Toasts*. San Francisco: Paul Elder, 1904.

Cohen, J. M. and M. J., eds. *The Penguin Dictionary of Quotations*. New York: Atheneum, 1962.

Collier, Carole. *505 Wine Questions Your Friends Can't Answer*. New York: Walker, 1983.

Collison, Robert and Mary, eds. *Dictionary of Foreign Quotations*. New York: Facts on File, 1980.

Colombo, John Robert, ed. *Colombo's Canadian Quotations*. Edmonton: Hurtig, 1974.

Columella. *Lucius Junius Moderatus Columella on Agriculture*. Vols. 1-3. Translated by E. S. Forester and Edward H. Heffner. Cambridge: Harvard UP, 1968.

Cooper, Arthur, trans. *Li Po and Tu Fu*. Baltimore: Penguin, 1973.

Copeland, Lewis and Faye, eds. *10,000 Jokes, Toasts, & Stories*. New York: Halcyon House, 1939.

Crashaw, Richard. *The Complete Poetry of Richard Crashaw*. Edited by George Walton Williams. Garden City, NY: Doubleday, 1970.

DeLoach, Charles, E., ed. *The Quotable Shakespeare*. Jefferson, NC: McFarland, 1988.

Dick, William B., ed. *Dick's Book of Toasts, Speeches, and Responses*. Danbury, CT: Behrens, 1883.

Dickens, Cedric. *Drinking with Dickens*. London: Mears Caldwell Hacker, 1980.

Dickson, Paul, ed. *Toasts*. New York: Dell, 1981.

Digby, Joan and John, eds. *Inspired By Drink: An Anthology*. New York: William Morrow, 1988.

Dow, Michael and Carl T. Endemann, eds. *Voices of the Vineland: An Anthology by Twenty-Two Napa Valley Poets*. Calistoga, CA: Alta Napa, 1978.

Drower, E. S. *Water into Wine: A Study of Ritual Idiom in the Middle East*. London: John Murray, 1956.

Duijker, Hubrecht. *The Wines of the Loire, Alsace, and Champagne*. New York: Crescent, 1981.

Dyce, Alexander, ed. *The Works of Beaumont and Fletcher*. Vols. 1 and 2. New York: D. Appleton, 1879.

Epictetus. *Epictetus: The Discourses*. Vol. 2. Translated by W. A. Oldfather. Cambridge: Harvard UP, 1928.

Etherege, George. *The Poems of Sir George Etherege*. Edited by James Thorpe. Princeton: Princeton UP, 1963.

Euripides. *The Bacchae of Euripides*. Translated by Donald Sutherland. Lincoln: U of Nebraska P, 1968.
———. *Euripides*. Vol. 3. Translated by Arthur S. Way. Cambridge: Harvard UP, 1912.

Evans, Bergen, comp. *Dictionary of Quotations*. New York: Delacorte, 1968.

Fadiman, Clifton, comp. and ed. *Dionysus: A Case of Vintage Tales About Wine*. New York: McGraw-Hill, 1962.

Fadiman, Clifton and Sam Aaron. *The Joys of Wine*. New York: Harry M. Abrams, 1975.

———. *The New Joys of Wine*. New York: Harry N. Abrams, 1990.

Field, Claud, ed. *A Dictionary of Oriental Quotations*. New York: Macmillan, 1911.

Field, Sara Bard. *The Vintage Festival*. San Francisco: John Henry Nash, 1920.

Frazer, James George. *The Golden Bough*. New York: Macmillan, 1922.

Gabler, James M., ed. *Wine into Words*. Baltimore: Bacchus, 1985.

Gajdusek, Robert E. *Hemingway's Paris*. New York: Charles Scribner's Sons, 1978.

Galen. *Galen on the Natural Faculties*. Translated by Arthur John Brock. Cambridge: Harvard UP, 1950.

Garrison, Robert L., comp. *Here's to You!* New York: Crown, 1980.

Gay, John. *The Poetical Works of John Gay*. Edited by G. C. Faber. New York: Russell & Russell, 1969.

Goodfellow, Adam, comp., and William Payne, ed. *A Book of Old Songs, Healths, Toasts, Sentiments, and Wise Sayings Pertaining to the Bond of Good Fellowship*. New York: New Amsterdam, 1901.

Gray, Arthur, ed. *Toasts and Tributes*. New York: Rohde & Hoskins, 1904.

Gwynn, Stephen. *Memories of Enjoyment*. Tralee, Ireland: Kerryman, 1946.

Ha, Tae Hung, ed. *Maxims and Proverbs of Old Korea*. Seoul: Yonsei UP, 1970.

Hafiz. *Fifty Poems of Hafiz*. Edited by Arthur J. Arberry. Cambridge: Cambridge UP, 1962.

———. *Odes of Hafiz*. Translated by Abbas Aryanpur Kashani. Lexington, KY: Mazda, 1984.

Hardy, Thomas K. *Pictorial Atlas of North American Wines*. San Francisco: Grape Vision, 1988.

Harris, Frank. *My Life and Loves*. New York: Grove, 1963.

Heintz, William F. *Wine Country: A History of Napa Valley, The Early Years: 1838-1920*. Santa Barbara, CA: Capra, 1990.

Henry, Lewis C., ed. *Toasts for All Occasions*. Garden City, NY: Garden City, 1949.

Herbert, George. *The Poems of George Herbert*. Edited by F. E. Hutchinson. London: Oxford UP, 1961.

Herrick, Robert. *The Poetical Works of Robert Herrick*. Edited by L. C. Martin. Oxford: Clarendon, 1956.

Hinkle, Richard Paul. *Central Coast Wine Book: from San Francisco to Santa Barbara*. St. Helena, CA: Vintage Image, 1980.

Horace. *The Complete Works of Horace*. Edited by Casper J. Kraemer, Jr. New York: Book League of America, 1938.

Hunt, Peter, comp. *Eating and Drinking: An Anthology for Epicures*. London: Ebury, 1961.

Hutchinson, William G., ed. *Songs of the Vine*. London: A. H. Bullen, 1904.

Hyams, Edward. *Dionysus: A Social History of the Wine Vine*. New York: Macmillan, 1965.

Hyman, Robin, ed. *The Quotation Dictionary*. New York: Macmillan, 1965.

Jobe, Joseph, ed. *The New Great Book of Wine*. Secaucus, NJ: Chartwell, 1982.

Johnson, Hugh. *The Story of Wine*. London: Mitchell Beazley, 1989.
——. *The World Atlas of Wine*. New York: Simon & Schuster, 1971.
——. *Vintage*. New York: Simon & Schuster, 1989.
——. *Wine*. New York: Simon & Schuster, 1972.

Juniper, William. *The True Drunkard's Delight*. London: Unicorn, 1933.

Kaufman, William J. *Champagne*. New York: Viking, 1973.

Kearney, Paul W., ed. *Toasts and Anecdotes*. New York: Edward J. Clode, 1923.

Keats, John. *The Poetical Works of John Keats*. Edited by H. W. Garrod. Oxford: Clarendon, 1958.

Kenko, Yoshida. *Essays in Idleness: The Tsurezuregusa of Kenko*. Translated by Donald Keene. New York: Columbia UP, 1967.

Khayyam, Omar. *The Rubaiyat of Omar Khayyam*. Translated by Edward Fitzgerald. New York: Crowell, n.d.

King, W. Francis H., comp. and ed. *Classical and Foreign Quotations*. London: Whitaker, 1968.

Koken, John M., comp. *Here's To It!* New York: Barnes, 1960.

Kressmann, Edouard. *The Wonder of Wine*. New York: Hastings, 1968.

Lamb, Richard and Ernest G. Mittelberger. *In Celebration of Wine and Life*. New York: Drake, 1974.

Laumer, William F., Jr. *About Wines*. Petersburg, FL: Great Outdoors, 1961.

Lausanne, Edita, ed. *The Great Book of Wine*. New York: Galahad, 1970.

Lawrence, R. de Treville, ed. *Jefferson and Wine*. Plains, VA: Vinifera Wine Growers, 1976.

Lesko, Leonard H. *King Tut's Wine Cellar*. Berkeley: B. C. Scribe, 1977.

Loftus, Simon. *Anatomy of the Wine Trade*. London: Sidgwick & Jackson, 1985.

Lolli, Giorgio, M.D., Emidio Serianni, M.D., Grace M. Golder, R.N., and Pierpaolo Luzzatto-Fegiz, L.L.D. *Alcohol in Italian Culture*. Glencoe, IL: Free Press, 1958.

Lowe, Paul E., ed. *The Twentieth Century Book of Toasts*. Philadelphia: David McKay, n.d.

Lucia, Salvatore P., M.D. *A History of Wine as Therapy*. Philadelphia: J. B. Lippincott, 1963.
——, ed. *Wine and Health*. Menlo Park, CA: Pacific Coast, 1968.

Madison, Janet, ed. *Toasts You Ought to Know*. Chicago: Reilly & Britton, 1908.

MacDonald, Kenneth and Tom Throckmorton. *Drink Thy Wine With a Merry Heart*. Ames: Iowa State UP, 1983.

Masefield, John, ed. *Lyrics of Ben Jonson, Beaumont and Fletcher*. London: E. Grant Richards, 1906.

Matthews, Patrick, ed. *Christie's Wine Companion*. Topsfield: Salem House, 1987.

Maynard, Theodore, comp. and ed. *A Tankard of Ale: An Anthology of Drinking Songs*. New York: Robert M. McBride, 1920.

Mencken, H. L., ed. *A New Dictionary of Quotations*. New York: Alfred A. Knopf, 1946.

Mendelsohn, Oscar A. *Drinking with Pepys*. London: Macmillan, 1963.
——. *Nicely, Thank You*. Melbourne: National, 1971.

Meyer, Justin. *Plain Talk About Fine Wine*. Santa Barbara, CA: Capra, 1989.

Mortlock, Geoffrey and Stephen Williams, eds. *The Flowing Bowl*. London: Hutchinson, n.d.

Mosher, Marion Dix, comp. *More Toasts*. New York: Wilson, 1932.

Mowat, Jean, ed. *Anthology of Wine*. Essex: W. H. Houldershaw, n.d.

Murphy, Edward F., ed. *The Crown Treasury of Relevant Quotations*. New York: Crown, 1978.

Muscatine, Doris, Maynard A. Amerine, and Bob Thompson, eds. *The University of California/Sotheby Book of California Wine*. Berkeley: U of California P, 1984.

Norman, Winston. *More Fun with Wine*. New York: Pocket, 1973.

Ousback, Anders, ed. *Words on Wine*. Melbourne: Holl of Content, 1977.

Ovid. *Ovid: The Erotic Poems*. Translated by Peter Green. New York: Penguin, 1982.

Parker, Robert E. *Place a Drop of Wine Near My Lips When I Die*. New York: Vantage, 1977.

Partnow, Elaine, comp. and ed. *The Quotable Woman: From Eve to 1799*. New York: Facts on File, 1985.

Peacock, Thomas Love. *The Works of Thomas Love Peacock*. Vol. 7. Edited by H. F. B. Brett-Smith and C. E. Jones. London: Constable, 1924.

Philippi, Donald, trans. *This Wine of Peace, This Wine of Laughter: A Complete Anthology of Japan's Earliest Songs*. New York: Grossman, 1968.

Plato. *Plato*. Vol. 5. Translated by W. R. M. Lamb. Cambridge: Harvard UP, 1925.

Pliny. *Pliny: Natural History*. Vol. 4. Translated and edited by H. Rackham. Cambridge: Harvard UP, 1960.

Pratt, James Norwood. *The Wine Bibber's Bible: A Practical Guide to Selecting and Enjoying Wines*. San Francisco: 101 Productions, 1971.

Prial, Frank J. *Wine Talk*. New York: Time Books, 1978.

Price, Pamela Vandyke. *Wine Lore, Legends, and Traditions*. Middlesex: Hamlyn, 1985.

Rabelais, Francois. *The Complete Works of Rabelais*. Translated by Jacques Le Clercq. New York: Modern Library, 1944.

Ramage, Craufurd Tait, ed. *Familiar Quotations from German and Spanish Authors*. London: George Routledge, 1904.

Ray, Cyril. *Lickerish Limericks*. London: J. M. Dent, 1979.
——. *Robert Mondavi of the Napa Valley*. Novato, CA: Presidio, 1984.
——. *The Guide to Wine*. New York: Exeter, 1978.
——, ed. *The Compleat Imbiber 5*. London: Vista Books, 1962.
——, ed. *The Compleat Imbiber 7*. London: Studio Vista, 1964.

Reeve, Lloyd Eric and Alice Means Reeve. *Gift of the Grape*. San Francisco: Filmer, 1959.

Reynolds, Cuyler, ed. *The Banquet Book*. New York: Putnam, 1902.

Roberge, Earl. *Napa Wine Country*. Portland: Graphic Arts, 1985.

Robinson, Jancis. *The Great Wine Book*. New York: William Morrow, 1982.
——. *Vines, Grapes, and Wines*. New York: Alfred A. Knopf, 1986.

Rogers, Cameron, ed. *Full and By*. Garden City: Doubleday, 1925.

Rosten, Leo, ed. *Leo Rosten's Treasury of Jewish Quotations*. New York: McGraw-Hill, 1972.

Rovira, Luis Rascala, ed. *Spanish Proverbs: A Survey of Spanish Culture and Civilization*. Lanham, MD: UP of America, 1984.

Saintsbury, George. *Notes on a Cellar-Book*. London: Macmillan, 1963.

Scarborough, William, ed. *A Collection of Chinese Proverbs*. New York: Paragon, 1964.

Schoenman, Theodore, ed. *Father of California Wine: Agoston Haraszthy*. Santa Barbara, CA: Capra, 1979.

Schoenstein, Ralph, ed. *The Booze Book: The Joy of Drink*. Chicago: Playboy, 1974.

Seaton, Jerome B., trans. *The Wine of Endless Life: Taoist Drinking Songs From the Yuan Dynasty*. Ann Arbor, MI: Ardis, 1978.

Seldes, George, comp. *The Great Quotations*. New York: Lyle Stuart, 1960.

Shay, Frank. *Drawn from the Wood*. New York: Macauley, 1929.
———. *More Pious Friends and Drunken Companions*. New York: Macauley, 1928.
———. *My Pious Friends and Drunken Companions*. New York: Dover, 1961.

Shelley, Percy Bysshe. *Shelley: Poetical Works*. Edited by Thomas Hutchinson. London: Oxford UP, 1967.

Simon, Andre L. *Drink*. New York: Horizon, 1953.
———. *Food*. New York: Horizon, 1953.
———. *The Commonsense of Wine*. New York: Pyramid, 1972.
———. *Wine in Shakespeare's Days and Shakespeare's Plays*. London: Curwen, 1964.
———, ed. *Wines of the World*. New York: McGraw-Hill, 1969.

Simpson, James B., ed. *Simpson's Contemporary Quotations*. Boston: Houghton, 1988.

Spenser, Edmund. *The Complete Poetical Works of Edmund Spenser*. Edited by R. E. Neil Dodge. Boston: Houghton, 1908.

Spurrier, Steven and Michael Dovaz. *Academie du Vin Wine Course*. 2d ed. New York: Macmillan, 1990.

Stevenson, Burton, comp. *The Home Book of Bible Quotations*. New York: Harper & Row, 1949.
———, comp. *The Macmillan Book of Proverbs, Maxims, & Famous Phrases*. New York: Macmillan, 1948.

Stevenson, Robert Louis. *Napa Wine*. San Francisco: Westwinds, 1974.

Sutcliffe, Serena. *Champagne: The History and Character of the World's Most Celebrated Wine*. New York: Simon & Schuster, 1988.

Taylor, Sidney B., ed. *Wine...Wisdom...&Whimsey*. Portland, OR: Winepress, 1969.

The Book of Common Prayer. Greenwich, CT: Seabury, 1953.

Thompson, Bob, ed. *California Wine*. Menlo Park, CA: Lane, 1977.
——, ed. *California Wine Country*. Menlo Park, CA: Lane, 1973.

Thompson, Bob and Hugh Johnson. *The California Wine Book*. New York: William Morrow, 1976.

Tovey, Charles, ed. *Wit, Wisdom, and Morals Distilled from Bacchus*. London: Whittaker, 1878.

Tripp, Rhoda Thomas, comp. *The International Thesaurus of Quotations*. New York: Thomas Y. Crowell, 1970.

Van Thal, Herbert, ed. *Belloc: A Biographical Anthology*. New York: Alfred A. Knopf, 1970.

Vine, Richard P. *Wine Appreciation*. New York: Facts on File, 1988.

Wagner, Philip M. *Grapes into Wine*. New York: Alfred A. Knopf, 1976.

Walsh, William S., ed. *International Encyclopedia of Prose and Poetical Quotations*. New York: Greenwood, 1968.

Wasserman, Sheldon and Pauline. *Sparkling Wine*. Piscataway, NY: New Century, 1984.

Waugh, Alec, ed. *In Praise of Wine: An Anthology*. London: Cassell, 1959.
——. *The Best Wine Last*. London: W. H. Allen, 1978.

Weinberg, Florence M. *The Wine and the Will: Rabelais's Bacchic Christianity*. Detroit: Wayne State UP, 1972.

Wemyss, Nina, ed. *Soul of the Vine: Wine in Literature*. Oakville, CA: Robert Mondavi Winery, 1990.

Wine Institute. *Wine in American Life*. San Francisco: Weiss, 1970.

Younger, William. *Gods, Men, and Wine*. London: Wine and Food Society, 1966.

Zraly, Kevin. *Windows on the World Complete Wine Course*. New York: Sterling, 1991.

AUTHOR INDEX

C

D

E

F

Join me now, dear friends of mine,
Raise a glass with me,
In love and laughter, share my wine;
May Bacchus set your spirits free!
                    Joni G. McNutt

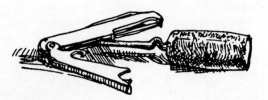